BEHAVIORAL

SYSTEMS

Robert L. Morasky

Artwork by
DAVID WACHS

PRAEGER

PRAEGER SPECIAL STUDIES • PRAEGER SCIENTIFIC

Library of Congress Cataloging in Publication Data

Morasky, Robert L., 1940-
  Behavioral systems.

  Bibliography: p.
  Includes index.
  1. Organizational behavior.   2. Behavior modifica-
tion.   3. Social systems.   I. Title.
HD58.7.M67 1982   658.3'14'019   82-12334
ISBN 0-03-062141-0

*Dedicated to James Morasky,
whose brotherly affection and generosity
made so many experiences possible for me.*

Published in 1982 by Praeger Publishers
CBS Educational and Professional Publishing
a Division of CBS Inc.
521 Fifth Avenue, New York, New York 10175 U.S.A.

© 1982 Praeger Publishers

23456789 052 987654321
Printed in the United States of America

ACKNOWLEDGMENTS

Several years ago Donald E. P. Smith and Dale Brethower introduced me to systems. Without their help, this book would not have the focus that it does. On the behavior modification side I owe a debt of gratitude to James M. Johnson, who provided both the information and the model for my development in operant psychology. Terry Schumacher, James McConnell, Hal Weidner, and Joseph McGrath deserve a special thanks for reviewing early drafts and providing the encouragement for me to continue with the project. Of course, there were the many graduate students who, having read early drafts, sometimes offered me explicit criticism of ideas and prose and at other times told me the notions and words were not right by simply not understanding. There were a number of typists—Carole, Lisa, and Karen—who magically produced the neat, printed copy from my nearly indecipherable yellow note pages. Finally, I am indebted to David Wachs for his creative efforts in designing and preparing the graphics, which add an indispensable dimension to the book. To all these people and to the many who made substantial contributions but have not been mentioned here, I extend my sincere appreciation and an offer to share with me the keen sense of accomplishment that comes with the publication of this book.

CONTENTS

INTRODUCTION

The central theme of this book is simply that planned behavior change always takes place within a structural and functional context that must be considered if the change in behavior is to be effective, efficient, lasting, and not disruptive to the environment within which the behavior occurs. A means for considering the context of behavior change, whether it be in a family, company, social program, or government agency, is a cross-disciplinary set of ideas loosely organized into a body of knowledge called the *systems approach*. It is the author's intent that the reader be able to understand the relationship between behavior change and the systems approach and be able to apply the concepts from each to the tasks of behavior management.

The audience for whom this book is written specifically includes behavior management specialists and in general includes anyone who works with people. The topic was limited to analysis and synthesis of behavioral systems, and examples of application were generally drawn from the area known as *organizational behavior management*. Let's look at each aspect of this book in some detail, beginning with the audience.

HOW CAN *BEHAVIORAL SYSTEMS* HELP BEHAVIOR MANAGEMENT SPECIALISTS?

Basically, the answer to that question is that the need for a systems framework seems to exist among behavior management specialists and the behavioral systems approach is complementary to the basic behavior management approach. Of course, that answer isn't always true, nor is it the case that specialists in other areas will not benefit from this book. However, in order to provide a consistent context for a look at the application of social systems analysis, *Behavioral Systems* is written with a slant toward those professionals who usually take a behavioral approach to problems. Throughout *Behavioral Systems*, references to *behavior management specialists* and *behavior managers* will be made interchangeably. In other literature, they may be called behavior modifiers or behaviorists or behavioral engineers. I think we are all referring to the same person.

It is assumed that behavior management specialists have (at a minimum) the skills to perform the following behavioral intervention tasks: analysis of behavior and identification of specific target behaviors, assessment of specific target behaviors, evaluation of baseline data, design of modification programs (including selection of contingencies, reinforcers, reinforcement schedules, and single subject research designs), implementation of programs (including data-based decision making), and evaluation of intervention programs.

These are the skills necessary for what Winett and Neale (1981) call *micro* level of analysis and management of behavior. Since we are assuming that behavior managers have such skills, there will be no attempt in this book to explain or elaborate on them. Nor will we focus on related issues such as behavior therapy or token economies. There are a number of good books available that emphasize behavior management skills at the micro or individual level. Five that I can recommend are: *Planned Behavior Change* (Fischer & Gochros, 1975), *Behavior Modification in Applied Settings* (Kazdin, 1980), *Behavior Modification: What It Is and How to Do It* (Martin & Pear, 1978), *Human Behavior: Analysis and Application* (Reese et al., 1978), and *Behavior Modification Procedure: A Sourcebook* (Thomas, 1974).

It is the intent of this book to introduce the behavior management specialist to systems because behavior management almost always occurs within a system and effective management requires an understanding of the system(s) within which the individual operates. This corresponds to Winett and Neale's (1981) *macro* level of analysis and management. This notion is explained in some detail in Chapter One, so further elaboration here would be premature. It is important to point out here, however, that regardless of the particular orientation taken, intervention with individuals (micro level) is facilitated by an understanding of the structural and functional context(s) (macro level) in which they work, play, learn, love, and compete. Students with cognitive, transpersonal, social (attitudinal), and even psychoanalytic orientations have benefited from classes in which this systems approach was taught. Furthermore, some of my favorite students have been business and engineering majors who are primarily concerned with nonbehavioral aspects of systems but who recognize the need to be able to deal with the humans behaving within systems. For those readers who do not view themselves as behavior management specialists, I encourage them to explore the application of systems concepts to their particular orientations. Application is possible, and it has been rewarding for others.

ANALYSIS AND SYNTHESIS OF BEHAVIORAL SYSTEMS???

Most system theorists would suggest that all systems behave, so what is so special about *behavioral systems*? (When system analysts describe the past or future performance of a system, they usually refer to the action as the "behavior" of the system.) In order to narrow down our field of study so that specific applications can be made, we will include only a limited type of system, the *behavioral system* within our category. Behavioral systems are those organizations, programs, groups, and so forth that are dependent upon the behaviors of the people within the system or that have a behavioral component that is critical to system functioning. Furthermore, although many species exhibit behavioral systems within larger systems, we will generally confine our discussion to human behavior. (After finishing *Behavioral Systems*, readers may enjoy examining the behavioral systems of bees. See Frisch, 1974.)

Examples of systems that are primarily behavioral include insurance companies, mental health treatment programs, educational and training programs, religious rites and ceremonies, government regulatory agencies, and hospitals. Instances of systems that are primarily nonbehavioral but that include a behavioral component are large-scale agricultural irrigation systems, water purification systems, assembly lines, and aircraft monitoring systems. You can see that the latter examples are generally mechanical in nature and if fully automated, can operate without a human behavioral component. This is not true for the former, which rely on human behavior but which may include a mechanical or technological component. Examples of nonbehavioral systems include such things as a light bulb, a black hole, an alpine fir forest, and the Yellowstone River watershed system. Only in a few instances will non-man-made or "natural" systems be used to illustrate principles in behavioral systems.

WHY USE ORGANIZATIONAL BEHAVIOR MANAGEMENT EXAMPLES?

When initially planning *Behavioral Systems*, I had in mind having several themes running through the chapters. However, a wise and highly published colleague suggested that one theme would carry the weight of concrete explanation better than three, and "Besides," he said, "organizational behavior management can subsume most of the parts of the other themes that you discuss." I think he was correct as long as organizational behavior management is defined to include systems as small as a three-person estate planning office and as diverse as a ranch, hospital, or federal regulatory agency. Thus, most of the examples throughout the book are oriented toward organizational behavior management, but the behavior management specialist who works exclusively with adolescent delinquents, biofeedback, Type A executives (especially them), or any of the other specialties that behavior management includes should realize that human behavior occurs in systems and that the basic concepts in this book will be relevant to diverse and even esoteric applications.

LITERATURE ON SYSTEMS

Throughout *Behavioral Systems*, the concepts and procedures of systems design, systems analysis, and general systems theory will be interpreted and defined so that behavior management specialists can apply them to the several tasks that they encounter. For the reader who would like more exposure to systems theory than occurs in this text, the following literature is recommended: *General System Theory* (Bertalanffy, 1968), *The Systems Approach* (Churchman, 1968), *Systemantics* (Gall, 1975), *Living Systems* (Miller, 1977), and *An Introduction to General Systems Thinking* (Weinberg, 1975).

AN OVERVIEW OF *BEHAVIORAL SYSTEMS*

Chapter One focuses on the system problems that behavior managers face and identifies four categories of problems or tasks that commonly necessitate an understanding of the larger context in which individual behavior occurs. Toward the end of the chapter it is suggested that a conceptual framework for behavioral systems may be a solution to the problem.

Chapter Two introduces a conceptual model for behavioral systems and discusses several basic concepts that are necessary yet not particularly complex aspects of the model. Even with the limited grasp of systems afforded by Chapter Two, a behavior manager will have some useful tools for understanding systems and enhancing behavior management programs.

Chapter Three establishes a rather rigid format for looking at whatever is used for evaluation and control of systems (we call them *goals*). Because very few real systems have goals that function adequately, the concept of system values is introduced in this chapter, and several observations about values operation are considered.

By the time the reader has reached Chapter Four, it should be apparent that behavioral systems do not operate in isolation but, rather, in chainlike arrangements that we call *external networks*. The necessity for understanding the various configurations and influences of external networks is emphasized in this chapter.

Chapter Five details some ways for grasping the essentials that make a behavioral system what it is. The topic is internal networks, or behavioral *sub*systems, and the focus is on the macro and micro arrangements within the system that permit them to function. Most experienced behavior managers assimilate the concepts of Chapter Five quite readily because they have seen the examples and have completed the analyses in real-life situations.

Chapter Six discusses feedback. Between applied behavior analysis and systems theory, there is an abundance of confusion about what feedback is or can be. An attempt is made to sort through the contradictions and jargon and to present a workable model of feedback in systems.

The importance of *needs assessment* becomes apparent in Chapters One through Six and is the topic of Chapter Seven. The first part of the chapter identifies what needs are from a systems standpoint, and the latter part explains a needs assessment procedure and provides a brief example of the approach.

Chapter Eight is devoted to a discussion of the analysis of behavioral systems. Of course, behavior management specialists will seldom perform a complete system analysis because that may not be necessary in order to operate an effective behavior management program.

Likewise, the complexity of systems prevents a planner from detailing every aspect of a proposed program or operation, but several critical parts must be elaborated in any design. The discussion of system planning and design in Chapter Nine should provide significant guidance for the reader confronted with the task of creating a system.

Chapter Ten is an assortment of odds and ends that may be written more for the author than for the reader. Some of the ideas there seemed important; others were just fun to think about. I hope that they stimulate the reader's thinking as they did mine.

Most chapters have two sections, each of which emphasizes different information. The material in italic is important to practical application and contains very little theory or explanation. It could be viewed as the "how to" or "so what" part. The remaining material delves into some theory, some examples, and a great deal of explanation. Readers can certainly obtain productive ideas from either of the sections, but if their interest is primarily application, they will find help in the italic portions of each chapter. If they want some background on systems, the areas that are not italic may be helpful.

ONE
THE PROBLEM

A BRIEF EXAMPLE OF THE PROBLEM

Lawrence Adams was educated at a Midwestern university in the field of personnel management and believed himself quite competent within his area of specialization. He joined Westronics Associates, knowing they had specific personnel problems. He was eager to combine his skills with the resources he was told were available at Westronics.

His first assignment was to remedy a problem that existed with two very important employees in the marketing department. They were both secretaries when they joined Westronics, but as the company grew, they evolved into part-time secretaries and part-time marketing and sales managers. Their job was to "flesh out" the skeletal outlines that sales representatives brought to them. "Fleshing out" usually meant producing complete equipment lists, estimated costs, production schedules, and first-estimate production plans. Recently, the term *plan developer* had been used to designate the position responsible for these tasks. Producing these items usually involved calling various companies or departments and/or digging the needed information out of technical manuals and tables.

The complaint to Adams was that the two plan developers were often a bottleneck because sales representatives could not finish proposals until the detailed outlines were ready. The chief marketing manager suggested that neither of the employees in question worked on an assignment from start to finish without working on several other projects in between and "never" without being reminded of the assignment set aside.

After some preliminary checking and conversations with the personnel involved, it seemed to Adams that it should be no problem getting a baseline of the time elapsed from initiation to completion of an assignment and subsequently reducing that time. He also decided to record and reduce the number of different jobs worked on between initiation and completion of an assignment. His intent was not to increase their overall output but just to decrease the "in-process" time.

The baseline data supported the complaints made to Adams. An average of 9.63 other projects were worked on between the initiation and completion of a specific project. The two secretary/management plan developers were shown the baseline data and asked to reduce the interfering projects to a level of 7.0. Adams had arranged for three different executives to check on the work periodically and to praise the two employees if the appropriate level was being met. A graph with baseline data and the target performance level was prominently displayed in the main office.

Difficulties began to surface immediately. The plan developers often had to call a subsidiary firm with engineering capabilities that provided crucial technical data. More often than not, the subsidiary firm gave the request a low priority and dealt with it when time permitted. Meanwhile, the plan developers worked on other projects. Adams asked the marketing manager to intervene with the subsidiary and get a shift of priorities. However, the subsidiary was not under the direct control of Westronics; hence, orders to change priorities had to come from elsewhere. Adams was assured that such a change was impossible. The subsidiary firm sometimes was part of the plan development process but usually was outside and independent of the plan development operation.

Adams further determined that the plans that required information from the subsidiary firm were not regarded as high priority by the sales representatives. The assistant marketing manager, however, believed that they should receive as high a priority as any other project. Adams was discovering that Westronics had some general purposes but that there weren't any specific directions that would help in determining priorities. Furthermore, Westronics had a number of different people directing operations and thereby controlling products so as to achieve different outcomes.

This brief example illustrates the relationship of total system configuration to individual behavior management. Since Adams did not have a framework for identifying the structure and function of the system called Westronics, the problems he encountered were not predicted nor avoided; to him Westronics remained a confusing, disorganized company.

THE UBIQUITY OF THE PROBLEM

During the late 1970s, a prominent communications company used the slogan, "the system is the solution." The position suggested here is that "the system is the problem." Although Adams was trained in psychology and specialized in changing human behavior, the situation he encountered at Westronics wasn't so different from what many professional psychologists and managers are encountering every day. The system somehow interferes with what needs to be done.

Systems problems not only affect those who manage behavior but also pose difficulties for technicians who focus on equipment that humans have to operate. Unfortunately, this latter group often does not perceive itself as being responsible for the behavioral aspects of the operation in question. If the behavioral system were recognized as a part of the total system, in many instances the desired outcomes would be achieved more easily. For example, environmental engineers design the mechanical and chemical aspects of a water treatment plant but seldom consider the human behavioral component that is necessary for the treatment plant to run. Of course, a fully automated plant really has no human behavioral system, but even in high technology fields complete automation is not the rule. By taking responsibility for coordinating the behavioral system with the rest of the system, more effective system performance can result.

A SECOND EXAMPLE OF THE PROBLEM

Let us consider an institutional situation involving a consultant who recognizes his responsibility for behavior management.

Dr. Renni is a psychologist who has specialized in the area of behavior management, or operant psychology. He teaches classes in behavior change and behavior therapy at a southern university as well as doing both basic and applied research. One of his applied projects involves working with Lincoln Hills Home, a church-supported institution for juvenile delinquent male adolescents. Renni spends about two hours a week consulting with Theresa Lund, who is the social worker/counselor at Lincoln Hills Home. Together they have done some remarkable things such as reducing Timmy's bed-wetting from an average of six nights per week to once in three weeks. Lorenzo got into fights at least once a day for two weeks; Renni and Lund established a program that reduced Lorenzo's fighting (he hasn't been in a fight in the last eight months).

However, the success in rehabilitating adolescent boys that the two professionals have experienced has not been without problems, and there is one type of problem that occurs repeatedly. Stated briefly, the problem is that "the institution won't support what needs to be done." For example, when Timmy's bed-wetting program began, Timmy was to be awakened at 11:00 p.m. and taken to the bathroom. He was also to be praised in the morning for a dry bed. When Renni saw no change in the frequency of bed-wetting after the first week of the program, he checked into the situation and discovered that on Monday, Wednesday, Friday, and Sunday, Timmy was not awakened and taken to the bathroom. Why not? Because the evening supervisor on those nights wasn't informed of his new responsibility. Why not? Well, the evening supervisors were college students who themselves were supervised by the assistant director on Tuesday, Thursday, and Saturday and by the resident social worker on Monday, Wednesday, Friday, and Sunday. The social worker had autonomy to conduct his own programs with the children in the home. He did not believe in behavior management approaches and, further, did not feel that evening supervisors should be a part of rehabilitation. As a result, the evening supervisors were not instructed to awaken Timmy at 11:00 P.M.

As Renni ferreted out the reason for the program not being carried out, he often thought in disbelief, "What kind of a show are they running here? How can you help these kids when everyone is doing his own thing?" He, of course, did not pose this question to the director of Lincoln Hills Home, but he did ask her what could be done to have the social worker comply with the treatment program. The director's response was, "I don't suppose we can do anything. The state regulations mandate that we hire a social worker. We give him the evening duties so he has something to do."

Renni eventuallly resolved the problem, and Timmy's bed-wetting decreased. Nevertheless, the initial difficulties were part of an encompassing entity that could be described as "Lincoln Hills Home as a system." Renni could not work with Timmy without working with the system.

As you can see from these two examples, some type of behavior change was intended in the case of both Lincoln Hills Home and Westronics, but it isn't only with direct behavioral intervention that the need to understand the system arises. Let's look at a variety of situations in which behavior managers encounter systems.

VARIATIONS OF THE PROBLEM

Behavior management specialists don't work just with cases where the major intent of the organization is to change individuals such as students in a school, inmates in a prison, or residents in a mental institution, although this is probably the primary thrust of their work. They also are called upon to change the behavior of employees of organizations, evaluate programs, and plan and design organizations. The "system is the problem" syndrome exists in all four circumstances.

Individual Change as the Major Focus

The example of Renni's work is an instance of behavior change of individuals being of major importance. Lincoln Hills Home was established to rehabilitate male juvenile delinquents. Boys who are residents of the home are there to have their behavior changed. Even if Lincoln Hills produced and sold furniture as part of an occupational therapy program, its purpose would not be to build or sell furniture but, rather, to develop appropriate behaviors through such a program. A behavior management specialist such as Renni may be called in to assist with a particular student or to be employed full-time to conduct an institution-wide behavior modification program. In either case, to achieve consistent, meaningful improvement in behaviors, the system(s) in which his clients exist must be taken into account.

Employee Change as the Major Focus

The example involving Adams illustrated the system problem when the behavior of an individual or individuals within the organization was to be the focus of the change. Westronics was the organization, or system, in question. Unlike Lincoln Hills Home, Westronics did not exist to change anyone's behavior; it built and sold electronic devices. In order to perform that function, individuals had to behave in certain ways. That was where behavior and behavior change came into the picture. Adams had to keep in mind that changing the behavior of the plan developers was only worthwhile if it improved production or sales. Behavior managers are often called upon to improve a situation through the modification of an employee's behavior (for example, see Quilitch, 1975), but, as the Westronics example illustrates, without an understanding of the system, the change can be more difficult than necessary, impossible, or even counterproductive.

Evaluation of an Organization

With the increasing interest in behavior management have come increased requests for behavior managers to evaluate programs and organizations such as community mental health projects, state police training and management, customer service departments, special education programs, transportation planning boards, assembly line management, social service delivery systems, and preschool day-care centers, just to name a few. It is one thing to point out a discrepancy between goals or objectives and actual achievements and quite another thing to pinpoint components, relationships, processes, subgoals, and feedback mechanisms that contribute to that discrepancy. In short, evaluation based upon a conception of the total system and its interacting networks is usually much more meaningful than a limited assessment of behaviors, contingencies, antecedents, and schedules.

A few years ago, the author was asked to evaluate a program within a mental institution. The request for evaluation was much more than just for a comparison of "what was" to "what was desired." To the institutional administrators, evaluation meant "identify what is," "identify what could be," "identify what should be," and perhaps, several other demands. Basic behavior management methodology would require one to list desired behaviors, assess behavior recording procedures, document contingencies, and compare performance to criterion levels and baselines. However, a relatively complete job of evaluation can be done when system concepts such as internal and environmental feedback, subsystem configurations, receiving systems, and internal and external networks are also taken into account.

Planning or Designing Part or All of an Organization

Whenever one prepares an application for a program development grant, that individual is creating a system. The person may not realize it or call it a system but nonetheless, that is what is happening. If the program to be developed involves change in human behavior or if humans operate in the program, it is a behavioral system. The success of the program will depend to a great degree upon the extent to which related programs and organizations are taken into account during program planning and the extent to which the program can adapt to existing conditions upon implementation. Taking existing and proposed systems into account will not necessarily guarantee success for a proposed program but system-based problems can be avoided by paying proper attention to system concerns.

For instance, consider *feedback*. Feedback loops are a system concern that many program developers ignore or forget to include when designing a system. As an example, the difference in effectiveness can be substantial between an executive decision-making training program that receives information about on-the-job decision-making performance and an identical program that does not receive such information. Feedback loops are not the exclusive domain of systems theory, but a planner with a systems orientation who plans a system without accommodations for feedback is unusual, indeed.

A PROPOSED SOLUTION

The behavior management specialist who has a general system framework to use when behavior modification, program evaluation, or program planning and design are needed will be able to avoid many of the problems caused by ignorance of "the system." Such a framework has to be basic enough to be easily understood and applied to diverse situations, yet complete enough to generate answers to critical questions. For instance, a general system framework for behavior systems should reveal:

- What are the purposes of the system?
- For whom?
- What are the parts?
- What are the relationships between the parts?
- How extensive is the system?
- What are the support mechanisms?
- How do you know when purposes are being met?

This is certainly not an exhaustive list of framework requirements, but it should provide a glimpse of what is needed.

The necessary behavioral system framework is the topic of the remainder of this book. It was derived from general systems theory, operations research, systems analysis, systems simulation, and cybernetic and systems engineering literature. Its focus is on application at a very practical level. Theory is introduced in order to explain a concept or to settle a disputed definition. Chapter Two will introduce a basic conceptual model of behavioral systems and provide the definitions to several crucial terms in the lexicon of the systems approach.

TWO
A CONCEPTUAL FRAMEWORK
FOR BEHAVIORAL SYSTEMS

Numerous authors have suggested the utility of the general systems approach to social systems, and several have provided either the rudiments for application or concrete examples of its operability (Berrien, 1968; Holder & Stratas, 1972; Laszlo, 1973; Laszlo, Levine, & Milsum, 1974). The potential that general systems theory and the systems approach hold for the analysis and synthesis of social systems appears to vary considerably, depending upon the specific needs of the user and the level of abstraction of the materials, framework, and model available. The intent of the framework illustrated in this chapter is to provide a concrete set of definitions and concepts that the behavior management specialist can readily implement. Other models or conceptual frameworks, such as Miller's "living systems" (1977) are available, but the experience of the author with behavioral approaches to systems has suggested the need for an applied conceptual framework. McConnell (1976) has established and implemented a rudimentary model, which he uses quite successfully with undergraduate behavior managers. The advantage of the conceptual framework presented here may be that it focuses less on individuals and their behavior as a system and more on individuals and their behavior as part of many other systems.

Figures 2.1 and 2.2 are schematic representations that can be the basis for behavioral system analysis. Obviously, social systems are not available on conference tables or under display cases for visual inspection, nor do they have the clearly delimited lines apparent in the models. The visual models in Figures 2.1 and 2.2 are not meant to be actual replicas of some existing physical presence but rather a conceptual framework that can be applied to the synthesis, analysis, and understanding of a behavioral system. This latter point is, perhaps, the major assumption underlying the

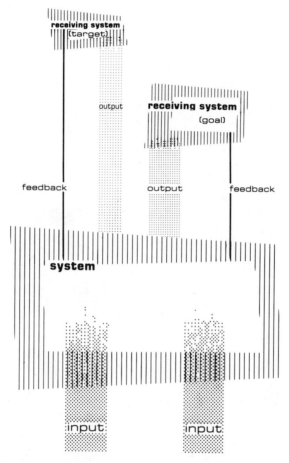

FIGURE 2.1   Behavioral system: external aspects.

ideas and procedures outlined in this chapter: the behavioral system model is composed of a valid set of discrete concepts derived from systems theory and related fields, which can be used by the behavioral scientist as a basis for directed analysis and/or synthesis of organizations.

Before dealing with the techniques of application of the model, it is necessary to comprehend the parts of the model and the implications for their existence and function. Some aspects of systems theory are clear-cut and reasonably agreed upon within the community of systems scholars. Other parts suffer from conflicting descriptions, internal inconsistencies, and insufficient analysis. The application of general systems theory to

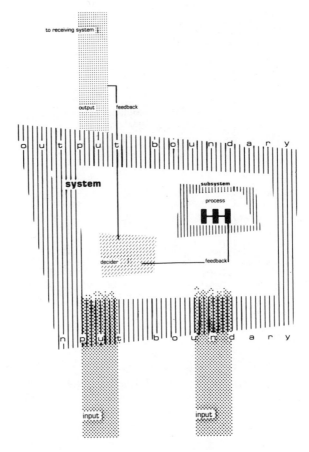

FIGURE 2.2   Behavioral system: internal aspects.

specific social problems has been hindered by the confusion arising from multiple definitions (DeGreene, 1970) and the "terminology jungle" (Klir, 1982) associated with the area. By explicitly defining the terms that are idiosyncratic to systems theory and by providing concrete examples, the present material should help to resolve some of the prevailing confusion.

In relation to the behavioral system model in Figures 2.1 and 2.2, the less ambiguous concepts are inputs, input boundaries, input ensemble, outputs, output boundaries, output ensemble, process, and interface. These will be discussed briefly in the remainder of this chapter. The other concepts identified in the behavioral system model will be dealt with in subsequent chapters. Unfortunately, the most basic of concepts, system, is somewhat ambiguous and also our necessary starting point. Before venturing into the quagmire of ambiguity, we should consider some jargon that will appear in later pages.

PREVIEW GLOSSARY

System: a structure of interacting animate and inanimate parts that receives inputs and produces outputs. Examples: police department, school, printing company, family, group, home, pediatrics ward.

Components: a general term referring to the parts of a system. Examples: the traffic and criminal bureaus could be components of a police department; parents are one component of a family—the mother and father are components of the component, parents, of the system, family (see Guideline 2.3).

Inputs: the things that enter a system. Examples: students are inputs to the system called school; manuscripts are inputs to a printing company.

Outputs: the things that leave a system. Examples: traffic citations are outputs from a police department; books are outputs from a printing company.

Process: the events that take place within the system to change inputs to outputs. Example: the medical treatment and care on a pediatrics ward between the time a child enters with an illness and leaves in good health is the process of that system.

Signal: a general label for the thing that is passing through a system. Examples: a patient in a medical clinic; an income tax report in an IRS office; a participant in a workshop; an inmate in a correctional center.

SYSTEM

Definitions of *system* vary widely in the literature of organizational and systems theory. Consider, for example, the following rather abstract statement: " . . . a nonrandom accumulation of matter–energy in a region in physical space–time, nonrandomly organized into coacting, interrelated subsystems or components" (Miller, 1965a).

And this straightforward version: "A system is a set of interacting functional relationships between various components which transform a set of inputs into a set of outputs" (Laszlo, Levine, & Milsum, 1974).

As the preceding quotes indicate, one need not venture far into the systems area before the formidable terminology jungle presents itself. What is a system? One has to begin a study of systems with the recognition that the English language may be inadequate to unequivocally define a concept that is applicable to many different disciplines. The definition needed must account for the atom, the lever, a hospital, the family, a rain forest, the heart, and an immense number of other phenomena as systems. Behavior managers, of course, don't need a universal definition. They need a description of systems that includes human behavior. As stated earlier, such systems will be labeled *behavioral systems* for the purposes of this book.

To the behavior management specialist, the concept, behavioral system, can best be thought of as a conglomerate or structure of animate and inanimate units, which through interaction receive inputs and pro- duce discriminable outputs. *Conglomerate* or *structuring* implies a non- randomness (Miller, 1965a) and a functionality or dimensionality of purpose (Angyal, 1941) that binds discrete units together. Consider the Westronics organization in Chapter One. It was a company (structuring) of employees (animate units) and resources such as machines, books, and electronic devices (inanimate units). The company received requests for information and proposals, orders, and (we suppose) customer comments (inputs) and produced plans, proposals, and electronic formats (outputs). Without a degree of unity of purpose, Westronics would probably look like a company in name only. Its unity of purpose gave Westronics a dimension that characterizes most systems.

The components of a system must interact or potentially interact in order for the system to exist. That is, a collection of people do not comprise a system until they act upon inputs and engage in purposeful processing of such inputs. All components need not act upon all inputs nor must the sequence of interaction be unchanging; hence, the notion that *potential interaction* is acceptable. Consider a particular college as a behavioral system whose function is to produce a specifiable output. A student progressing through the system will interact with some of the professors and some of the library books but not with others, yet still become part of the specified output, oftentimes regardless of the order of interaction. Each professor or library book remains a component of the system with potential for interaction with any student.

Without inputs and outputs, a body of units is not a behavioral system as far as the behavior management specialist is concerned. The purposefulness of the behavioral system necessitates that it produce something; hence, it must have outputs.

However, one might ask, "What about organizations that seem to produce something, but that 'something' is difficult to define or specify— are they systems?" Remember, it is often the behavior manager's job to clarify the outputs of a system, especially those involving rehabilitation or behavior modification, and development of this skill should be part of that person's training. If, while collecting information on a supposed system, the behavior manager comes to the conclusion that the group outputs nothing, inputs nothing, and apparently has no specifiable purpose, the verdict is inevitable; in that individual's framework it is not a system. Of course, the individual who is suspicious at this point might do well to explore the public relations work of the group to determine if its major output is information about its existence as a system. In an age of complex tax legislation and self-serving organizations, it is not ludicrous to expect to find a system whose purpose is to convince its environment that it is a system.

Contrary to other definitions of systems (Berrien, 1968), a system for the behavioral system specialist need not demonstrate the occurrence of change between inputs and outputs. It appears at first that any organization that simply outputs exactly what it inputs is purposeless, and as suggested above, is not a system. The author does not object to this reasoning, but in order to take in such systems as libraries, data banks, and human communications relay teams, it is most convenient to set aside the "change" requirement and stress purposefulness in its place. Otherwise, storage systems are systems only if the output is different than the input in terms of its new position in time (which is never constant). A similar condition exists with transportation systems, which alter only the input's position in space before it becomes an output.

OUTPUTS

Individual products, or *outputs* of a system, taken as a group, are often called the *output ensemble*. Few systems have a single output, and as a result, the behavior management specialist confronting a system should be prepared to compile a frequency-rank-ordered list of outputs. That is, various outputs of a system are more likely to occur more often than others within a given time span and, therefore, can be ranked higher on the output list or ensemble. For example, consider a family counseling program that has several outputs ranging from custom budgeting and buying on the low-frequency end to advice on specific child management problems on the high-frequency end. The output ensemble could be rank ordered as follows.

Output Ensemble for Family Counseling System (arranged highest to lowest frequency)

1. Verbal advice on specific child management problems
2. Written family planning information
3. Lecture presentation on behavioral approaches to child management
4. Referrals to marriage counselors
5. Customized family budget and buying guides

The ensemble above illustrates only the nature of each output but does not include specific statements about quality nor is any mention made of quantity other than the relational one implicit in ranking. A complete system design or analysis would include quality and quantity data.

Completeness requires that the behavior manager be alert to a variety of products coming from a system in various modes, which could be part of the output ensemble. In addition, the task of making the output description as specific as possible is important, much as is the case with instructional design and behavioral objectives (Mager, 1965). For example, a mental health clinic director might claim that family counseling is the only goal of the clinic and that the only output is people (family members) who have participated in group counseling sessions. Yet, the clinic secretary claims to spend 30 percent of her time preparing instructional material to distribute to community service groups. The instructional material coming from the clinic must be considered an output, and the possibility exists that proportionately fewer "group-counseled" people are outputs than are instructional materials.

Outputs need not be intentional system products. That is, often a system will output products that were not a part of its original or explicit purpose. For instance, "waste" products such as empty ice cream containers are often emitted from school lunch systems as a necessary, yet unintentional, aspect of the system's functioning. In another instance, fear or distrust of psychologists could result from unpleasant experiences in an undergraduate psychology class and, therefore, be an output of that system, although the system did not intend to develop such behaviors in its students.

Unintentional system outputs often are selected by other systems that were not originally identified to receive the outputs. With the proper feedback, the system producing the unintended outputs can be influenced by the unintended receiving system to maintain, decrease, or increase the flow (a later discussion will relate to this situation).

The ideal, well-designed arrangement, of course, is one in which clearly identified outputs are produced to become intended inputs for some other previously identified system. It is not unusual, however, for a number of outputs from a system to be "not selected" as inputs for another system. These nonselected outputs are part of the output ensemble even though the previously identified receiving system does not input them. For example, suppose a drug rehabilitation unit (system) outputted pamphlets about their work to specific church groups, but those groups did not read them nor do anything with them other than to leave them in their mailing packets on the shelf. The pamphlets are a part of the drug rehabilitation unit's output ensemble and are also nonselected outputs.

What happens, you might ask, if in the situation above another group discovers the pamphlets and makes use of them, that is, accepts them as inputs? Are they still considered nonselected outputs? Yes, in the framework described here, they are. The other group that discovered and made use of the pamphlets was *not* the previously identified, intended receiving system. The church group did select *not* to input the pamphlets, so they remain in the nonselected output category.

INPUTS

If a system is to produce outputs, whether intentional or otherwise, it must take in materials with which to operate. The signals, information, energy, and so forth entering the system are called inputs and are collectively labeled as the *input ensemble* (Miller, 1965a).

There is little controversy over what an input is. Once a signal has passed into a system and is part of the system process, it is an input. However, some difficulty can arise when one attempts to describe an input. For example, if 47 mothers apply to a social welfare agency for child-care support, it is incorrect to list 47 females as an input. The women were not the actual things being processed by the system. Their applications for child-care support funds were the inputs relevant to the functioning of the system. Even if the women carried their files from office to office and interview to interview, the input being processed is still the application, not the human transporting it.

This distinction between the body or structure transporting a signal that the system can process and the signal itself becomes important and, perhaps, confusing when one considers such systems as correctional institutions. If a prison is simply a system for incarcerating human bodies with particular behavioral histories, then, indeed, the input is just "a human body." If, on the other hand, the system has some reduced level of recidivism or continued criminal offenses as a goal and its intended outputs are ex-inmates with revised behavioral repertoires, then it is inputting more than just a body. It is necessary in this case to describe the input in terms of its excessive or deficit characteristics just as it would be necessary to describe the process as something more than storage and the output as more specific than "paroled individuals." The institution is, in fact, going to process and output a human whose physical structure was not the reason for that person being an input. Therefore, the input description should not be simply "X number of male/female persons." The input ensemble should describe what the system is actually taking in for processing, not the apparent structure that might only be carrying the signal.

The previous social welfare and prison system examples illustrate the difference between behavioral systems that only require behavioral interactions to achieve a nonbehavioral purpose and those that require behavioral interactions in order to change some *behavior*. In the former group are such systems as water treatment plants that input impure water, output potable water, and in between, include the behaviors of several humans to achieve the change. Insurance, accounting, and other financial agencies also input nonbehavioral signals such as applications or information for estate planning. Through a sequence of behavioral interactions, a nonbehavioral product such as an audit report, a proposal, or a policy may be outputted. The behavioral sequences in these examples are critical to appropriate functioning of the system although the system itself may be viewed as primarily mechanical, chemical, or financial.

On the other hand, systems such as mental hospitals, schools, prisons, rehabilitation centers, and clinics not only have specific behavioral sequences to convert inputs to outputs, but the inputs and outputs themselves are also behaviors.

Considering that we are calling systems such as water treatment plants behavioral systems if they contain a behavioral sequence, it would seem appropriate and, indeed, desirable for civil engineers to be skilled in the analysis and design of the behavioral aspects of an otherwise nonbehavioral operation. This undoubtedly holds true for many types of systems and system designs that are viewed as primarily physical, chemical, mechanical, or otherwise nonbehavioral.

BOUNDARIES

There seems to be little question but that systems do have boundaries of some sort (Easton, 1961; Emery & Trist, 1960), yet few authors spend much time describing or clarifying their nature. This could be due to the relatively simplistic nature of the concept, compared with other aspects of general systems theory. The definition given by Berrien (1968) is applicable to most cases in which the concept is used: "The boundary is that region separating one system from another; it can be identified by some differentiation in the relationships existing between the components inside the boundary and those relationships which transcend the boundary."

The boundaries of a behavioral system need not be a physical entity identifiable in a consistent time and place. They can shift, be conceptual in nature, and exist in several ways and places at the same time. The *input boundary* can be viewed as that imaginary plane through which a signal passes when moving from being a potential input to being an actual input of a system. For example, as one stands silently before an emergency room receptionist, one is outside the boundary of that system. As the receptionist looks up, recognizes the presence of a human, says, "What can I do for you?," listens to your problem, and replies, "A doctor will see you in a moment," one has passed through the boundary and become a signal within the system. The receptionist's office is not exactly the boundary of the system nor is the receptionist nor were her words, yet in combination, all of these were parts of the boundary. Had you arrived unconscious in an ambulance and had the emergency room personnel removed you from the ambulance, the boundary would have been in a location different from the receptionist's office, and some aspect of your physical condition would have been part of the boundary.

Another approach to system boundaries is to assume that they exist in an identifiable place during certain times and that the *conditions* under which they operate can be specified. For instance, it is accurate to say that one part of the emergency room system boundary resides at approximately the receptionist's desk between the hours of X and Y. The boundary conditions at that point during those times are that: (1) one potential input can be processed at that time, and (2) those potential inputs that display life-endangered symptoms will be permitted to cross the boundary and become inputs.

The description given above identifies one of the functions of the boundaries that Berrien (1968) discusses; namely, that boundaries control the rate of both input and output flow. The other important function was that of coding and decoding inputs. The role of the receptionist in the example above can readily include the coding-decoding function. For example, a heart attack victim who collapses before the receptionist's desk is likely to give rise to a coded call for aid that most visitors to the hospital would not recognize as, "There is a patient in emergency that is possibly a cardiac arrest case."

It seems apparent that boundaries also serve the function of turning away potential inputs that the system cannot or will not process. In that sense, the boundaries control the quality and quantity of inputs and outputs as well as coding and decoding the signals. The person who is not demonstrating life-endangered symptoms will not be treated in the emergency room described above. The conditions existing at the input boundary will not permit that person to become an input. In a similar manner, the conditions existing at the output boundary will not permit a person to leave the emergency room or become an output until certain requirements have been met.

PROCESS

There appears to be little dispute over the nature and definition of the concept, process, as it relates to systems. Regardless of whether one chooses the "process-product," "structure-function," or the "means-ends" distinction, the process remains as that activity that occurs within the boundaries of the system. As the quotes below indicate, it may be labeled as the system *procedures* or *flow*, but the concept remains the same.

Hodge (1970) is undoubtedly referring to process when he mentions "the transformations from input to output." Somewhere and somehow within a behavioral system an input is changed to become an output. The sequence of behaviors that act upon the input to produce an output is the process.

When Beishon (1972) discussed the components of a system and the connections between components being links, he was probably talking collectively about the process of that system. In a similar sense, DeGreene (1970) describes a system network design that "shows more detailed interrelations between the subsystems, indicating how the system is formulated from the basic requirements." If one has a system network design, then it appears that one would also have at that time a scheme of the process of the system. The use of the term *network* is consistent with the definition given by Miller (1965a), namely, that it is the complete set of channels connecting components. Networks will be discussed extensively in later chapters.

When referring to state and process descriptions, Simon (1969) very elegantly characterized them as "the warp and weft of our experience." Processes, according to Simon, are the means by which outputs having desired characteristics are produced.

If one cannot observe the goings-on within the boundaries of a system, than the process of the system is said to be in a "black box" (Ashby, 1958; Beishon, 1971). This simply is a means of saying that the system exists, its inputs and outputs are identifiable, but we cannot determine what is occurring between the input and output boundaries. The black-box designation is unusual in the analysis or synthesis of behavioral systems because it is generally possible to identify the actions taken and decisions made in such systems. This is not to say that it is easy. The task of tracing an input through the maze of a social welfare agency, for example, with its myriad of alternate channels, given various conditions, can be a major headache, but not impossible.

Before going on we need to preview a few words that will appear on the next few pages.

PREVIEW GLOSSARY

Subsystem: that portion of a larger system that carries out a specific task or function. Examples: the traffic bureau is a subsystem of the system, police department; the "meal preparation operation" is a subsystem of the system, family.

Suprasystem: the next larger system in which a system is embedded or nested. Examples: if the surgery ward is the system being examined, city/county hospital is the suprasystem; if the sales management section is the system being examined, then the marketing department is the supra-system.

Receiving system: the system to which outputs go. There may be several receiving systems for a given system. Some receiving systems may be labeled "intended receiving systems" to indicate that the intent of the system was that outputs would flow to a specific or "intended" receiving system. Examples: subscribers and readers are the receiving systems for the system, daily newspaper; community families are the receiving systems for fire safety instruction (output) from the system, fire department.

Input Source System: the source from which a system gets its inputs. Examples : a police department (system) gets requests for assistance (inputs) from the community (input source system); a land use planning committee (system) gets petitions (inputs) from business (input source system); an electronic diagnosis training program within a company gets students from franchised agencies.

INTERFACE

At first glance the concept *interface* would appear to be a less complicated issue than many of the other aspects of systems; however, this is not the case. Although it is not extensively nor specifically discussed in current literature, the use of the term varies considerably. Take, for example, E. Laszlo's (1972) description of subsystems as coordinating interfaces whose function is to "pull together the behavior of their own parts, and to integrate this joint effort with the behavior of other components. . . ." Berrien (1968) might agree with Laszlo's use of the term since he identifies the interface of two systems as the region between the boundaries of two systems. In contrast, however, to this notion of the interface as a "between-systems region or system" is the concept of interface as a point or plane where two systems meet or make contact (Beishon, 1972; Simon, 1969). If the output boundary of one system is seen as contiguous with the input boundary of another system, then those systems are said to "interface" at those boundary surfaces that make contact. The actual difference between the two foregoing definitions seems minimal, but the ramifications are considerable.

If you accept the former concept of interface as a region between system boundaries, then you should consider the question of how interface is different from system. Berrien (1968) makes the argument that the interface, unlike the system, shows no interaction between parts. Therefore, the signal that is traveling through or across the interface must not be altered, but he also states that the interface can be a system that, by his own definition, means that the output will be different from the input. Interface is obviously one of the more confusing concepts in the behavioral systems framework.

Observation of social systems seems to support the idea of an *interface system*. Take, for instance, a birth control information center that mails pamphlets to newly married couples. The postal service is clearly not the intended receiving system, nor is it within the boundaries of the birth control center. It serves the function of a distribution system and as such, could be labeled as an interface system.

In spite of such convincing examples, there are reasons why one might avoid defining interface as a region between systems. If such a definition is accepted, then the universe is not an interlocking, hierarchical network of systems, subsystems, and suprasystems. Somewhere in that universe are the voids between systems that we should account for in some manner. To call them interfaces and claim that they are in some cases systems and at other times functionless and, therefore, not systems, does not adequately allow for meaningful application of the concept.

On the other hand, conceptualizing the interface of two systems as a plane corresponding to output/input boundary contact also raises some serious questions. Even viewing the interface as the point at which outputs of one system become inputs for another system does not account for variations in system arrangement. A particularly disturbing problem with the latter definition involves the idea of entropy. *Entropy* is the label given to a situation where matter, energy, information, and so forth, moves from an ordered to a less-ordered state (Parsegian, 1972). A less-ordered state is a more random state. In the case of energy and information, less-ordered or highly random states are less useful than are more-ordered states. If an output of one system is not accepted by the intended receiving system, it becomes a nonselected output. Nonselected outputs deteriorate over time; that is, they become less ordered and, hence, less useful. As Berrien (1968) claims, they become waste. However, they are not within the boundaries of the system that produced them nor have they entered the boundaries of the receiving system. They are in the region between the systems and the logical name for an area "between the faces of the systems" would be interface. At least one author (Berrien, 1968) has suggested that interface accepts waste; that is, entropy remains in what he called the interface.

A solution to the dilemma of having incompatible concepts of interface is to assume that all systems are, in fact, interlocking and overlapping. Therefore, it must be concluded that regions or voids between systems cannot exist, but, rather, that these areas are themselves systems. Henceforth, in the behavioral system model, the point of actual contact where an output becomes an input or vice versa will be the interface (*and the boundary*), while those systems between the initial system and its receiving system will be called *intervening systems*.

The postal service is an intervening system between letter writer and recipient, as is a library between author/publisher and reader and a trucking company between producer and consumer. It may not always be the case, but most intervening systems will only change the input's location in time or space before making it an output. That is, such systems will not alter any aspect of the input other than to move it from one place to another or to store it for some period of time.

It follows, then, that systems that do not have output-input exchange do not interface with each other. Furthermore, should entropy of outputs increase between the system and its receiving systems, whether resulting from nonselected outputs or natural deterioration, the intervening system will accept and retain that waste just as any other system would. It does not follow, however, that all storage in an intervening system is entropic. The intervening system could present a signal with full fidelity to the intended receiving system after a lengthy period of storage.

THE BASIC CONCEPTUAL FRAMEWORK
AND THE BEHAVIOR MANAGEMENT SPECIALIST

Having waded through a swamp of terms such as inputs, outputs, boundaries, and processes and having fallen into an interface pit full of hungry contradictions, you deserve some recapitulation while sitting comfortably on a sunny hammock. We started this discussion in Chapter One by identifying four situations that can be problems for the behavior management specialist. At the root of the problem was the influence a system may have on contingencies or on the behavior of individuals within the system. The behavior manager can anticipate and avoid these *system problems* if an understanding of the critical systems is gained beforehand. Perhaps the most useful approach to this type of understanding is to have on hand a framework for behavioral systems that can be applied whenever the previously identified situations occur. An applied behavioral system framework was introduced in Chapter Two.

So what do we have now? Well, suppose an eight-agent real estate firm asks you to consult on a motivation/management improvement program. Although you may previously have had the skills to identify individual behaviors to be increased or decreased and to suggest reinforcement procedures for management to implement, you now also have a basic framework for understanding the real estate firm as a system in which the behavior will occur. Let's elaborate on this example.

By asking the owner/manager, Ellen Beaman, a few directed questions, you may discover a rather elaborate output ensemble that includes offers to purchase property, refusals to sell property, descriptions of property, bank loan applications, property transfers, subdivision proposals, property appraisals, prospecting calls and letters, employee paychecks and government paperwork. Inputs include offers to purchase property, refusals to sell property, descriptions of property, requests for information about property, requests for closing aid, requests for appraisals, commission payments, and regulations about government paperwork. You recall something called *process*, so you ask a few questions about how things get done around Valley Land Office (Beaman's real estate firm). It doesn't take long to realize two important things: (1) three separate processes seem to operate at Valley Land Office according to the type of input received—one seems to deal mostly with farm and ranch property, another deals exclusively with business and industrial properties, the third restricts itself (or is restricted) to residential property, and (2) Beaman is aware of the existence of three different processes but does not perceive the differences in critical behaviors, behavior chains, contingencies, and reinforcement schedules.

Well, you have already learned a great deal about Valley Land Office that will help you immensely when a behavior management program is implemented, but you have one more concept from Chapter Two that you haven't used yet—interface. Valley Land Office is a system so it probably interfaces with other systems. Which ones? How? If you learned that the agents in the residential properties process had established a number of seemingly important interfaces with systems that provide prospects and that that was an important part of their success, you might want to consider that when Beaman says, "You need to do something with our industrial market. If it did as well as the residential agents, we'd be overloaded with work."

Even without the basic system framework from Chapter Two, you may have to set up contingencies to increase specific behaviors within the three distinct processes and differential contingencies to shift the rank ordering of various outputs, and you may even have increased the number of prospects through reinforcement of contacts (interfaces), but the chance of missing an interfering factor and running smack into a system problem was minimized because you had a framework from which to work. Suppose there had been another process in the Valley Land Office that dealt with appraisals of farm, industrial, and residential property. It obviously would cut across the other apparent divisions of interest, and without appropriate consideration as a distinct operation within the office, its existence could hinder the success of your motivation program. You were able to help Beaman and Valley Land Office more than you might have otherwise because you understood them as a system and worked within the existing system structure. In some cases where it made sense, you might have even suggested changes in the system to promote a more effective process and outcome. You undoubtedly would have heard the comment from the Valley Land Office agents that systems specialists often hear, "It's remarkable . . . You've only been here a couple days and you seem to know what's going on as well as (or better than) we do."

With your help, Valley Land Office is now functioning better than it was . . . or is it? Perhaps during the preceding discussion of your imaginary consultant work you asked the question, "Just what am I trying to change?" A *motivation/management improvement program* could be aimed at a number of things. It definitely is not axiomatic that the Valley Land Office agents would be motivated to sell more property or that Valley Land Office would experience improved management in order to increase corporate profit. "Why else would you do it?" you ask. Well, Beaman may want to simply maintain the current level of business and increase Valley Land's influence on land-use policies and practices. It is critical for you to comprehend the direction, aim, goal, objective, or purpose of a system before you attempt to change behaviors of those individuals within the system. What are system goals? No doubt you have encountered definitions of goals or objectives before and are confident that similar notions should apply to systems. Perhaps they do, but the next chapter on system goals and values may have some surprises for and may even give you a new way to look at organizations.

CHAPTER TWO: GUIDELINES
FOR PRACTICAL APPLICATION

Guideline 2.1: *If managing, evaluating, or changing individual behaviors, seek out the larger context (system) in which behaviors occur (are supposed to occur). Look for: system inputs and outputs, input sources, input boundaries and conditions, output boundaries and conditions, and interfaces. Use the examples in the table at the end of this section for reference. The material in that table is not meant to be complete but, rather, instances of the things for which we look.*

Guideline 2.2: *Look for conflicts or discrepancies between aspects of the system and the behavior to be changed. Look for things that may be supporting the inappropriate behavior.*

Guideline 2.3: *To avoid some of the frustration arising from the nesting of components (that is, systems have components; components can be viewed as systems, therefore, they have components; systems are parts of larger systems, therefore, they are components themselves and so on and so on . . .), select the thing that you need to look at as "the system" and identify the components only down to the level where they cease to have a substantial impact on the process and outcomes of the system. The same advice applies to the suprasystem—system—subsystem notion. Once you select the level or operation to be examined, call it "the system" and analyze up (supra) or down (sub) only to those levels that have a substantial impact on purpose or function of "the system."*

Guideline 2.4: *The advice given in Guideline 2.3 applies to a vertical analysis but is equally useful in a horizontal analysis. Once you select the operation to be examined, call it "the system," call the system on its input side the "input source system," and call the system on its output side the "receiving system."*

—Remember that every system is potentially an "input source system," "the system," and the "receiving system." What they become in your analysis

depends upon your perspective, that is, it depends upon which system you chose to be "the system."

—Remember that if (after starting an analysis) you change the label "the system" from one system to another, the labels "input source system" and "receiving system" will also change. Avoid making such changes without specific recognition that you are doing so.

Examples of Behavior Management Tasks and Some General Items to Identify

Behavior Management Task	System	Inputs	Outputs	Input Sources	Boundaries and Boundary Conditions	Interfaces
Decrease the frequency of incorrectly written citations and improper arrests	Police department	Calls for assistance, directives, public criticism, training	Citations, warnings, reports, assistance	Administrators, citizens, newspapers, instructors, other officers	Precinct, city limits, on-duty/off-duty, appropriate requests for assistance	With schools, justice personnel, fire dept., highway dept., federal law enforcement agencies

Decrease the frequency of accidents in the assembly section of a company	Production department of furniture manufacturer	Product specifications, quotas directives, invoices, raw materials	Finished products, reports, complaints, contracts, waste products	Other plants, administrators, other departments	Limits of the assembly site, quality control specifications	With distributor, supplier, unions, federal regulatory agencies, community offices
Increase nurse consultations with doctors and patients	City/county hospital	Patients, directives, prescriptions, drugs, standards	Healthy individuals, corpses, reports, waste products, records	Emergency room, doctors, administrators, regulatory agencies, pharmacy	Ward or floor limits, age, nature of illness, supervisor's desk	With other hospitals, clinics, police, ambulance service, federal and state agencies, employee organizations

THREE
SYSTEM GOALS AND VALUES

SYSTEM GOALS

A casual perusal of organizational theory and program planning literature should quickly lead one to the conclusion that goals can and, in the opinion of some authors, should be an integral aspect of organization or program operation. If one pursues the information available regarding goals, another conclusion will begin to emerge: not everyone agrees as to what goals are. More specifically, there are those authors who refer to goals as if a priori knowledge of the nature of a goal were available to all readers, and there are other writers who assert that specific things are true of goals, yet these same writers ignore the truths about goals put forth by other authors, and vice versa. There are references to public goals, private goals, internal goals, external goals, supergoals, subgoals, and even non-goals and mongols. In short, one is often assured by authors of the necessity of goals without being clearly informed of the definition of the thing that is so necessary. This situation leads to a variety of conditions for organizations and programs, the most common of which seems to be that goals are often haphazardly derived, poorly understood, and limited in function.

The intent (or goal) of Chapter Three can be stated as follows: upon completion of the chapter, you will be able to derive, comprehend, and employ goals for specific functions in program planning, design, and analysis. In addition, you should have a good grasp of a "slippery" concept called *system values*.

Parts of this chapter were taken from R. L. Morasky, "Defining Goals: A Systems Approach," in *Long Range Planning*, 1977. *10*. Copyright 1977 by Pergamon Press, Ltd. Reprinted by permission of Pergamon Press, Ltd.

If a behavior management specialist employs goal statements or develops system designs that are purported to be goal oriented, the following discussion should be relevant. Initially, two questions will be considered: What are the functions of system goals? and What are the characteristics of system goals? Having answered these two questions, a definition of goals will be stated and illustrated with concrete examples. As was the case in previous chapters, there are some terms that need brief explanation before we continue.

PREVIEW GLOSSARY

System Network: a string or sequence of systems connected by input/output flows. At the minimum, such sequences include the system under examination, the input source system, and the receiving system. There is no maximum number of systems that can be interconnected. Example: parts of a "beef production network" include the feeder lot as the system under examination, ranches as the input source systems, and meat packing houses or slaughterhouses as the receiving systems.

State Variable: a part of a system that can assume different values. Examples: state variables of a prison could be inmate population (350 minimum to 800 maximum), number of guards (105 minimum to 270 maximum), and number of recreation minutes per week for inmates (0 minimum to 21 hours maximum).

System State: a condition displayed by a system that is usually associated with one or more state variables. Examples: a real estate sales system could be in state A wherein it has more than 100 residences for sale or in state B wherein it has less than 100 residences for sale; a family could be in state A wherein arguments occur nightly, in state B wherein arguments occur weekly, or in state C wherein arguments occur on the average of once a month.

System Goal: a manifest statement that describes the specific state a receiving system should attain by a specified time. Goals facilitate evaluation and control of systems. Examples: for a fire department, within 12 months the community will have 40 percent fewer fires than the average for the past 5 years; for a job training program, within 12 months, community businesses will employ 12 of the 15 adolescents currently being trained.

Target: an outcome or state that a system is approaching that is not described in the system's goals. If the system has no goals, all outcomes that it approaches are targets. Examples: a system may be set up to increase citizen participation in land-use planning but actually outputs materials that bias citizens against mobile home subdivisions (target); a system may be designed to increase the number of small businesses owned by minority group individuals in a community (goal) but actually increases the size of existing medium-sized businesses owned by nonminority group individuals (target); a government agency without goals may be doing little more than increasing its budget, its staff, and its record file (targets).

Feedback: information coming to a system about various state variables within the system and within receiving systems. Examples: officials of a prison (system) may get information (feedback) about the number of parolees (outputs) gainfully employed (state variable) in a particular community (receiving system); a manager (subsystem) of a department store (system) may get information (feedback) about the number of sales-clerks (state variable) and special sales (state variable) during rush hour.

Functions of System Goals

Goals are often considered to be a critical part of the system evaluation process (Crowder & Bennett, 1976; Holder & Stratas, 1972; Yuchtman & Seashore, 1967). The degree of system effectiveness can be judged if a goal for system direction has been previously established. Since evaluation is typically a match-to-sample or match-to-criteria process, the judgment rendered in system evaluation is based upon a comparison of attained system state to desired system state. The desired system state is also the goal. Therefore, it seems apparent that one function of goals is to facilitate evaluation by providing criteria for attained state and desired state comparison.

If we assume that social systems are created for specific reasons or purposes, then it follows that planning and creating social systems implies a measure of control. Since evaluation and control go hand in hand and goals are necessary for evaluation, it must follow that control of a system is facilitated by goals. This can be illustrated most clearly with the concepts of cybernetics, as described by Parsegian (1972), or feedback according to Miller (1965b), which are integral parts of systems theory. In order to control the behavior of a system or organization, it is essential that information about the outputs or their influence on the environment be available to the person directing the system. This information feedback can be compared with desired levels or effects, and corrections can be made to increase or decrease the outputs and their influences on receiving systems. The desired levels or effects can be derived from established goals. Therefore, the procedure for controlling a system is one of evaluation followed by alterations in system behavior, based on the results of the evaluation. As previously stated, evaluation is facilitated by goals; hence, control must also be facilitated by goals.

Goals, then, can be viewed as having at least two major functions for system or organizational planning and management: (1) they can facilitate system evaluation and (2) they can facilitate system control.

Characteristics of System Goals

Criticisms aimed at the use of goals and goal-setting models for improving organizational effectiveness are often based on poorly developed concepts of the nature and function of goals, but this is to be expected when a standard set of attributes for the concept, goal, does not exist. Even in a book such as Mager's *Goal Analysis* (1972), there is not a list of concrete, definitive, acceptable characteristics to which a goal should conform. It is not surprising, then, that many programs and organizations find goals to be everything and nothing, the supposed orientation of the system but, at the same time, meaningless statements. Meaningfulness is, of course, relative to one's viewpoint; however, if we accept the concept that goals have the functions identified previously, certain characteristics become necessary.

First Characteristic: Focus on Receiving System

An initial attribute of a goal that begins to give it meaning is its focus. Consider the situation for a moment from a systems theory standpoint: a program, organization, or system is to be developed or revised; thus, goals are to be set. Where should the goals be focused? On some part of the system itself? Or on some aspect of the system's environment? Several authors (Beckett, 1971; Haberstroh, 1965; Rosenbleuth, et al., 1943; Summerhoff, 1969) strongly suggest that goals relate to the system's environment rather than to the system itself. The logic of such a directive is apparent if you recognize two basic assumptions of systems theory. First, the universe can be conceived of as a network of interacting, interconnected systems. Second, social (and behavioral) systems are open, that is, they receive inputs and produce outputs. An implication of the first assumption is that there is no "space between systems." As we discussed in Chapter Two under *interface*, systems connect with each other to form networks. Therefore, the environment of a system must be other systems with which it interacts. It can interact with other systems in only two ways;

it can receive inputs from other systems or send outputs to other systems. It follows then that the environment of a system is composed of the *input source systems* and the *receiving systems*. An implication of the second assumption is that things called outputs do, in fact, leave the system. Putting the implications together will result in the conclusion that outputs from social systems must flow to receiving systems that are inextricably influenced by those outputs. The influence on the receiving system is inevitable in open system configurations; therefore, it should be the *focus of the system goals*. It follows, then, that goals facilitate evaluation of system effectiveness, *relative to the receiving system*.

If a goal simply describes a desired state for *the system* and not its environment, the goal will, in most cases, deal either with some aspect of the process *the system* is to utilize or the outputs it is to produce. Holder & Stratas (1972) state very clearly, however, that "Goals are not the methods (program activities) devised to achieve these goals." In light of the concept of *open systems* presented above, it seems rather ludicrous to set as an end for which the system functions that it will exhibit a certain process, although in some counseling and therapeutic approaches this is certainly done. It seems equally ludicrous for evaluation of a system to focus on the system's process rather than on the outcome, but this is also done (McInnis & Kitson, 1977). Such an operation brings to mind the gadgeteer or home mechanic who puts gears, cams, levers, pulleys, and switches together simply to operate with no final purpose in mind for the system other than to have its parts turn, move, or switch as they were intended. The output in such a case, along with the effect on the receiving system, remains unspecified. This is not an acceptable situation for social systems in which goals are to be functional. The goals must be focused elsewhere than on the process that is to be carried out.

In addition, the goals of organizations or systems should be more than just the production of so many outputs of a certain type or quality. The relationship between goals (which focus on the receiving system) and outputs is a logical one, based initially on inference. That is, if the system is designed with a well-defined goal relating to the receiving system, then the outputs of the system are those products that, by inference, seem to be necessary to achieve those goals. If, on the other hand, a system designer or manager ignores the receiving system and says that "the goal of X system is to output Y number of Z products," he is implying that, regardless of the usefulness of Z products or the effects of Z products on the environment, the system still has as an alleged goal the outputting of those products. In such a case the system is usually considered to be goal oriented if some portion of the Y number of Z products is being outputted, and the goal can be considered reached if Y number of Z products has been produced. You might say, however, "Be reasonable, the designer set that goal because the environment or receiving systems *needed* Y number of Z products. He isn't going to design a system that produces something that isn't needed or won't be purchased." And that is just the point! If the environment or the receiving system *needs* a certain number of a specific product, the goal of the system is to satisfy that need, *which could be achieved by outputting the proper products.* The goal of the system is to effect a change in the receiving system's state. When that change has occurred, the goal of the system has been achieved. To repeat an earlier statement: if the system is designed with a well-defined goal relating to the receiving system, the outputs of the system are those products that, by inference, seem to be necessary to achieve those goals.

Second Characteristic: Specificity

A second characteristic of goals that seems to be commonly accepted is specificity (Haberstroh, 1965; Holder & Stratas, 1972; Mager, 1972). The gathering of quantitative and qualitative data to evaluate a system's effectiveness is possible only if the goals of the system are clear and unambiguous. Unfortunately, goals are highly susceptible to that scourge of evaluation that R. Mager (1972) calls "fuzzy thinking." A vague, nonspecific goal is of little use to the behavior management specialist or system manager because any number of states can be construed to be appropriate to goal attainment. In order to make a goal optimally useful for evaluation, the statement of the goal must be painfully specific.

The notions of *system states* and *state variables* are important to our discussion at this point. A system *state* is the condition or configuration that a system is exhibiting at a particular time. For instance, a simple system such as a light switch is either in the state "off" or "on." More complex systems can display a greater range of state values than the two associated with "on-off" systems. *State variables* are those aspects of a system that can be identified, measured, and assigned values or states. Consider, for example, the state variable, input rate, for a three-magistrate judicial system that is designed to deal only with bankruptcy cases. Assume that the input rate of cases could vary from zero per month to thirty per month, and assume further that the current system state for the state variable, input rate, is 11.5 per month. If you were designing goals for a judicial reform program, you might select as a goal that "the judicial system handling bankruptcy cases will increase its input rate from 11.5 per month to 24 per month." A specific state variable and specific system states have been identified and utilized in the goal statement. The resulting goal is sufficiently objective to permit evaluation of the effectiveness of the judicial reform program relative to its receiving system, the judicial system handling bankruptcy cases.

Third Characteristic: Time Dimension

The goal stated above pertaining to the judicial system has a noticeable deficit that, by omission, illustrates a further characteristic of adequate goals, that is, it has no time dimension. When will the input rate be increased to 24 per month? In two months? Two years? How can one evaluate the effectiveness of a system with relation to goals if one doesn't know when to apply the criteria? Similarly, can system managers control a system if they don't know how it should be behaving at a particular point in time? Of course, they can evaluate system effectiveness and control system direction without explicit temporal checkpoints but their decisions are based upon a value structure that might not be shared by all who deal with or operate within the organization.

On the other hand, if a goal statement is specific, focused upon receiving systems, and contains a time dimension, subgoals that operate as checkpoints for evaluating and controlling the progress of the system toward the established final goal can then be established. For instance, a resources system that supplies materials to an assembly system must know exactly which materials and how much of each one will be needed by the assembly system in order to maintain an effective total organizational network. Furthermore, the resources system must know when the assembly line must have the materials in order to evaluate how successful they have been and to control the proper level of resources outputted to the assembly system. It is one thing to say, "The assembly group will need 400 frames, 400 cross members, and 800 support beams," and quite another to say that 20 percent of the items will be needed 6 months from today, 40 percent will be needed in 8 months, and so on.

Fourth Characteristic: Goals as Manifest Statements

The final characteristic of goals that must be present if they are to serve the two functions of evaluation and control is one that deals more with the attachment of the goal to the system than with the actual structure of the goal statement. Yuchtman & Seashore (1967) refer to it as the functional approach to organizational effectiveness that amounts to the question of whether or not people know what the actual goal of the system is. Organization charters, policy statements, and meeting minutes are often of little use in ascertaining goals. System analysis techniques can reveal data that can be used to infer directions of an organization or system, but if no one in the organization can provide a specific statement that has a time dimension and is related to the receiving system, how does anyone know what the goals of the system really are? The answer is arbitrary and simple: unless the goal statements are manifest, you assume that the system has directions (which we will discuss later under *targets*) but no goals. You should take the position that goals function to facilitate evaluation and control and that unless the system has manifest statements that exhibit the proper characteristics, the system must be considered to be operating in the absence of goals.

What is a *manifest goal*? Certainly a system that has written statements called *goals* could be considered to have manifest goals. (Remember, however, that unless the other three characteristics are also present, the written statements could not be used for evaluation and thus, in our terminology, would not qualify as goals.) We would also say that the requirement of being manifest was met if there were no written goal statements but if every member of the system identified the same goals verbally. Obviously, in this latter case, the goals had somehow been made public, which is an adequate measure of manifestness.

You will often encounter systems in which some members will claim that the goal is one thing and others will claim something else. It is then up to you to determine if goals have been set and made public (perhaps by simply asking, "How do you know that is the goal?").

Although the present discussion makes this matter appear to be a tricky, fine discrimination to make, in fact, it is a rather obvious condition in most situations. You will have little difficulty in determining whether or not the goals of a system have been communicated to the members of the system.

Definition of Goals

System goals are manifest statements describing the specific state a receiving system should attain by a specified time. Goals facilitate two functions of organizations or systems: (1) evaluation of program effectiveness relative to receiving systems and (2) control over system behavior. In order to provide such facilitation, goals must exhibit four characteristics. They must: (1) focus on the receiving systems, (2) be specific enough to permit objective interpretation, (3) specify a time dimension, and (4) be manifest statements.

Each characteristic is necessary for the existence of a goal but is not sufficient in itself. All four characteristics must be present to establish that a functional goal exists. Statements purporting to describe system direction that do not exhibit all four characteristics should be viewed as directional statements with limited function. A system operating with such statements should be viewed as moving toward targets. Evaluation and control of target-oriented systems should be viewed as based upon value structures, not upon goals. The latter portion of this chapter will deal with such a situation in some detail. Meanwhile, let us take a concrete look at goals.

An Example

To further illustrate the importance of well-written goals to controlled system functioning, let us ignore one or two of the goal characteristics described above and, using a concrete example, identify the effect that such contravention has upon function. Suppose a system was planned based upon goals that were specific, manifest, and had a time dimension but focused upon the system itself rather than the receiving system. The following situation is representative of such goal development.

A small-plot agriculture system (SPAS), funded by a national government agency, has as its receiving system those families residing on tracts of land with 2 to 20 arable acres. The designer/planner of the SPAS drafted the following goals:

Goal #1: Within 45 days of its establishment, the SPAS will have a 90 percent completed list of the names and locations of families residing on appropriate land tracts within the SPAS district.

Goal #2: Within 90 days of its establishment, the SPAS will conduct a workshop on "Small-Plot Agriculture."

Goal #3: During the initial 12 months of its operation, the SPAS will conduct 4 workshops dealing with planning, establishing, managing, and harvesting small agricultural plots.

It is apparent that these three goals are specific enough for objective evaluation, contain a time dimension that permits temporal control, and are manifest. However, none of the goals relate to the state(s) of the receiving system. Note that, if the SPAS is viewed as the receiving system for *some other system*, all three statements meet the criteria for goals for the *other system*. In this light, these statements are appropriate goals for the subsystem managing, that is, inputting into, the SPAS but are not appropriate goals for the SPAS itself.

Keep in mind that the SPAS will output to those families residing on tracts of land with 2 to 20 arable acres. It is entirely within reason to imagine that the SPAS could accomplish all three ends identified in the statements above, that is, "have a list," "conduct a workshop," and "conduct 4 workshops" and not change the state of the receiving systems. The three goal statements for the SPAS, as prepared by the system designer/planner, do not provide for evaluation of the effectiveness of the SPAS with relation to its receiving systems. Consider the following revised goal for the SPAS:

Goal #4: During the 1978 growing season, 75 percent more acreage will be utilized for small agricultural plots by the families in the SPAS district than was used in 1975.

Goal #4 is one that will function adequately within the systems framework. (It is assumed that the term "small agricultural plot" is defined operationally elsewhere.) The previous three statements might be descriptions of the actions that the SPAS will take in order to attain Goal #4, but, conceptually, they are the process of SPAS, not the goals.

Let us consider a modification of Goal #4 in which the specificity is removed. Suppose the designer/planner feels that specific amounts in goal statements guarantee failure; therefore, in order to avoid jeopardizing his reputation, he drafts the following, "During the 1978 growing season more acreage will be utilized for small agricultural plots by the families in the SPAS district than was used in 1975."

By eliminating the reference to a specific percentage increase, the designer/planner has made it impossible to objectively evaluate and control the effectiveness of SPAS; hence, the goal is no longer functional. A 100-acre increase in total acreage utilized could certainly be construed as "more," but if that increase already occurred during the 1977 growing season, has the goal already been met? Or should efforts be made to make the increase greater? Why? Because someone's value structure dictates that something more than a 100-acre increase is desirable? If the goal statement included the 75 percent designation, and if the 1977 increase constituted a 25 percent increase, SPAS would need to accelerate its efforts to achieve the projected end state. Another way of viewing the situation is that the 25 percent increase in 1977 is information feedback to the management of SPAS. The input, process, output, or some other aspect of SPAS would need to be altered in order to effect a 75 percent increase by 1978. Such is the manner in which goals can be used to facilitate the evaluation and control of systems.

The small-plot agricultural system example makes an assumption about goals and evaluation obvious which has been implicit thus far. Goals are projections into the future. Further, they are working projections from which decisions and directions are generated. They are not absolutes that spell doom and failure for the designer/planner if they are not met. Neither the designer/planner nor the system are "bad" if goals are not achieved. One must simply accept that the system's effectiveness in relation to the goal is less than desirable. If the variables impeding system effectiveness are known and under the control of the system manager, adjustments can be made and effectiveness can be increased. If such variables remain unknown, then at least for the moment, a realistic view of the system is possible.

Summary

Goals are indigenous to many planning procedures, but their function and structure are often not explicit. By defining goals, from a systems theory standpoint, two functions and four definite characteristics can be identified; goals should serve to facilitate the evaluation of system effectiveness and the control of system behavior. In order to provide this facilitation, goals must be specific, manifest, focused on the receiving system, and must include a time dimension.

Systems Operating in the Absence of Goals

As a practicing behavior management specialist, you will quickly discover that very few organizations have goals that conform to the characteristics identified above. The most difficult organizations with which to work are those that claim to have goals or objectives but that actually have goallike statements that are focused inappropriately, are nonspecific or that have no time dimension. Such systems usually are doing something quite different from what your interpretation of their goallike statements would indicate. If time and energy permit, you may choose to determine what the actual targets are and to help management see the discrepancy between stated direction and actual direction. Only when that discrepancy is erased, can you set up behavior management programs that will contribute to system effectiveness. As you might guess, this is no small task.

On the other hand, working with an organization that doesn't even have approximations of goals will also cause some headaches. In spite of the difficulty involved, the behavior management specialists can work with and understand a system without goals if they apply some basic notions about values. Before we expand on the concept of system values, we should consider definitions for a few more terms.

PREVIEW GLOSSARY

Decider: the part of every system that performs the management or executive function, such as determining input/output boundary conditions, process, feedback mechanisms, and component selection. (Keep in mind that the decider is an activity or function, not a person.) The decider function can be (and often is) performed or shared by more than one individual. Examples: the decider function of a prison determines the type and number of inmates entering the prison, the treatment received by inmates in the prison, the type and number of parolees released from the prison, and the number and type of staff employed within the prison. Note that some of the decisions in the prison example would be made by the warden, some by the parole board, some by judges passing sentence, and some by government officials such as the governor.

System Values: the hierarchy of preferred system and receiving system states. Such values reside with the decider function and may or may not coincide with goals. Examples: the three supervising nurses (decider function) of the geriatrics ward (system) often seem to prefer that the patients be lying down and nondisruptive during social hour (value) rather than ambulatory and engaged in discussion (goal); the social workers (decider) in an urban nutrition improvement program (system) without specific goals seem to prefer that the clients (receiving system) eat three times a day (value A) more than other outcomes, such as eating balanced meals (value B) or eating natural or unprocessed foods (value C).

First Order Receiving System: the receiving system that inputs directly from the system in question.

Second Order Receiving System: the receiving system that receives inputs from the first order receiving system. A second order receiving system is once removed from "the system." Examples: a jobs training program (the system) may output graduates with basic skills to a technical training center (first order receiving system), which in turn will output these same persons to a job setting (second order receiving system); a law firm (the system) may output tax law interpretations to a financial advisor (first order receiving system), who will in turn use the information to output financial plans for clients (second order receiving system).

SYSTEM VALUES

It has been suggested by a number of system and organization theorists that social systems have values. Consider the following quotes:

> The main point of reference for analyzing the structure of any social system is its value pattern. This defines the basic orientation of the system . . . to the situation in which it operates . . . (Parsons, 1956).

> These functional prerequisites, including the value pattern, are universally present in every social system (Yuchtman & Seashore, 1967).

> A system develops a preferential hierarchy of values that gives rise to decision rules which determine its preference for one internal steady state value rather than another (Miller, 1965).

A behavior management specialist who is trying to grasp the operation of an organization should keep in mind the preceding statements, but what exactly is the value pattern of an organization, agency, program, or any other form of social system? In what specific ways should system values be taken into account?

Structure of System Values[*]

It might be well to begin by establishing a definition of values, and then move to speculations about the function of such a system component. In his research with individuals, Rokeach (1973) identified two types of values, *terminal* and *instrumental*. These value types can also be applied to systems. Terminal values can be regarded as preferred *end* states while instrumental values can be viewed as the preferred *means* for achieving end states. A value structure, then, would be the rank-ordered arrangement of the values, both terminal and instrumental, of a system. If this rather straightforward description of values is combined with the systems theory concept of open or interacting systems forming networks, it results in a system value structure that must include consideration of the various states of the system's environment as well as the system itself.

If systems do indeed interact, then the effect of one system's outputs on the states of another system must become part of the value structure of the first system. Theoretically, a system can rank order any set of end states according to preference of occurrence. *This is not to say that each and every system* has already formulated such a ranking nor that states of equal preference would not appear, but, given a choice between State A or State B, State B or State C, and so on, it is assumed that a system manager could identify preferences and hence, a rank-ordered list would evolve. This means that the value structure of the system in question would include possible end states for both the system and the receiving systems to which its outputs were being transmitted. Of course, the actual rank ordering of these end states would depend upon the particular system in question and would quite probably change over time. That is, it would be expected that certain end states pertaining directly to System A could rank either higher or lower on the value structure of System A than would certain end states of the receiving systems of System A. Add to this value

---

[*] Several authors have questioned the advisability of attributing concepts such as goals and values to organizations or systems that are essentially abstractions (Cyert & March, (1963). Even while trying to avoid the notion of a "group mind" in systems, J. D. Thompson (1967) put forth the idea of a "domain consensus," which, like system values, seems to be a readily recognizable aspect of system behavior while at the same time is dependent upon the perceptions of those behaviors for existence. That is, it is the action of the system that permits its observers to come to some judgment of the domain within which the system functions, and it is those same actions that allow the observer to conclude that one end state or means to an end is preferable to another. Hence, whether it has a "mind" or not, a social system or organization can be said to have values by virtue of the behaviors and preferences for displayed ends.

structure certain instrumental values that are preferred to certain terminal values, and the result is a mixture of more or less desired end states for two or more systems and more or less desired means for achieving the end states.

Note that the notion of system values as presented here is much like that of goals; however, a crucial difference does exist. Among other things, goals must be specific and manifest in order to be functional. Values operate even if they are implicit and not manifest. From this standpoint goals can be manifest values, although this need not always be the case.

Let us examine a concrete situation that may clarify the description of value structures. Consider a local agricultural improvement program such as was discussed earlier under the section on goals. If such a social system had no clear-cut goals, system values would direct the performances of the system toward what we call *targets*. Those targets or values would include desirable end states for the system itself, as, for instance, "having within the extension service a computer facility programmed to predict grain and seed costs."

It would also have values related to the end states of the systems that receive its outputs, for example, "farms with 200 or fewer acres will produce at least 4 different vegetable types."

Further, certain instrumental values would be a part of the value structure, such as, "the preferred means for making contacts with farm operators is through a community meeting mode."

Thus, it is apparent that this agricultural improvement program could have a value structure that gives it various priorities to: (1) its own possible end states, (2) possible end states of other systems, and (3) possible means for achieving end states.

Operation of System Values

While previously introducing the example of the agricultural improvement program, it was assumed that, since the system had no clear-cut goals, the behavior of the system would be influenced by the values of the system. This assumption could bear a closer look. As was established earlier, if goals are to be used for evaluation and control of a system, they must be specific, manifest, have a time dimension, and be stated in terms of the state of the receiving system. Of course, goals with other functions (such as simply guiding the system) could have other characteristics (Young, 1966). Nevertheless, each of the four characteristics mentioned is a necessary, yet not sufficient, condition for goals if they are to function as facilitators of evaluation and control. All four characteristics must be present for sufficiency.

This rationale for suggesting that all four characteristics must be present in order for goals, and not values, to function relies heavily upon the assumption that social systems have an executive component that Miller (1965b) has labeled the *decider*. The decider function of a system controls many aspects of system functioning including system process, input and output rates, and boundary conditions. If the decider function has a set of system goals that are specific, manifest, stated in terms of the receiving system, and include a time dimension, it can control system operation with relation to those goals. Removal of any of the characteristics from a goal would result in the decider function being forced to apply a set of internally housed standards to judgments about system functioning. That is, given feedback about outputs and their effects on the environment, the decider can determine whether or not these outputs are appropriate by applying parameters from goal statements. However, if goals do not exist, are vague, or are focused inappropriately, the decider must choose to continue or change outputs by matching current conditions with criterion conditions that he must generate from his value structure.

Goallessness and Directionlessness

Should a goalless system also be considered directionless? Certainly not. As long as outputs are produced, the system has behavior and direction, although it may not be consistent, adaptive, or stable. This is the first point at which the behavior manager must be aware of system values and their importance to successful behavior management within the system. If a decision is made to create a system that does not have adequate goal statements, it should be done with full realization that the decider function of the system will make decisions about the operation of the system, based on a value structure. There is no currently accepted theory of rational decision making that does not presume some pre-existing terminal or instrumental value structure. Therefore, the goalless system, no matter how well planned, will function according to the values of the decider function. In fact, a system with goals could also function according to the values of the decider if the decider rejects the stated goals and chooses to base its decisions regarding the system on an implicit value structure.

But back to the case of the goalless system—is this situation so undesirable? Why not let the decider function direct the system once general guidelines have been set? On the surface, this arrangement appears rather attractive because it provides for the possibility of rapid adaptation to environmental conditions impinging upon the system. This could very well happen, but let us consider a different approach before jumping to conclusions.

Values and Reinforcers

Having introduced the concept of the decider function into the discussion, it is an appropriate time to confront an opposing viewpoint. Skinner would argue that values are an unnecessary construct for the description of systems. "Any list of values is a list of reinforcers— conditioned or otherwise" (Rogers & Skinner, 1956). In the language of operant psychology, reinforcers are stimuli that increase the rate or probability of occurrence of behaviors that they immediately follow. In the language of systems theory, these reinforcers or stimuli are information coming to the system in the form of external feedback from the environment (Miller, 1965a). Skinner (1953), himself, has referred to reinforcers as "feedback." In both the systems theory and operant psychological approaches, the stimuli or feedback are considered to relate to the effect the behavior or the system output has on the environment. That is, whether viewed as stimuli or information, feedback from the environment provides the decider with knowledge about the state of the environment, subsequent to behavior or outputs from the system. If it is accepted that the environment of a system includes those systems receiving inputs from it (Hall & Fagan, 1968, pp. 81–92), then feedback from the environment or, if you prefer, reinforcement, is information to the decider regarding the state of receiving systems. Again, it can be assumed a priori that the decider will hold certain states as more preferable than others; hence, a value structure or reinforcer hierarchy can be assumed to exist. In the systems sense, hierarchies of reinforcers are value hierarchies and vice versa. One does not subsume the other nor are they in a subordinate-superordinate relationship. They are mutually substitutable constructs.

A necessary distinction must be made, however, between system values as operationally *active*, "revealed" preferences for certain end states or means to ends and as *beliefs* about preferred end states. In the former situation values and reinforcers coincide, but in the latter case one set of beliefs about a system's value structure could be held and expressed while the functional set of reinforcers could be quite different. The relationship of system behavior to reinforcers and the reliability of the measurement procedure have been well established in the applied behavior analysis literature. Unfortunately, the same circumstances do not prevail with survey methods of assessing values (Hughes et al., 1976; Rokeach, 1973). Although survey methods may appear more efficient than other approaches, their efficacy has yet to be demonstrated.

THE RELATIONSHIP OF
GOALS, VALUES, AND TARGETS

We have been discussing three concepts, system goals, values, and targets, which are similar in nature and often confusing in their inter-relationships. A brief explanation should help to clarify the differences among them. The notion of system goals and their functions and characteristics should be quite clear by this time. It should also be fairly clear that when systems do not have goals, they continue to operate and that systems values are the basis for deciding what will be done. Further, the directions or ends that the system seems to be approaching are the system targets. Unlike goals, targets focus on any part of the system or its receiving system(s). A system can have goals *and* targets.

We know if a system has goals because they must be manifest. Once we identify goals or once goals are established (if a system is being planned), succeeding conclusions about system outputs or processes are deductively inferred. Essentially, the logic runs as follows, "If Goal A is to be achieved, then Output X and Process Y are necessary."

On the other hand, we can only know system targets by inductively inferring them from identified system values or from observed outcomes over time. Whereas there is a great deal of certainty associated with goals because of the requirement of manifestness, the opposite is true for targets. They generally are not manifest and in order to identify them, we must use limited observations or limited information about values; thus, it is difficult to say with certainty, "System A has as a target the achievement of State 2 in Receiving System B."

Let us look at a concrete example that emphasizes the relationship between values and targets. A city/county land-use agency is the system under examination. It has no goals. Its purposes, as stated in the minutes of the meeting in which it was created, are to develop a master plan for land use in the county and to provide recommendations to the land-use commission on proposed building projects. These stated purposes may or may not have something to do with system targets; only information from observations will establish that. As it turns out, the director of the city/county land-use agency is verbally in favor of maintaining the ecological balance and environmental quality of the air, water, soil, traffic, and aesthetics of the county. The record of his recommendations to the land use commission supports the validity of his statements. Even in the face of pressure from council members, commissioners, and land developers, his agency thoroughly investigated proposed construction and fought vigorously for protection of the environment.

On the other hand, the city/county land-use agency has done practically nothing on the master plan. It seems that the method that the director insists upon for making master plan decisions calls for extensive collection and analysis of data on environmental variables. The agency has not had the employees necessary to carry out the investigatory work. Observation would indicate that the two parts of the master plan that are completed were done exceedingly well and are exceptionally well-documented.

Based on the comments of the director and the observations of recommendations and master plan work, we can inductively infer two targets, based upon the values of the city/county land-use agency. First, the agency seems to value the county in a rather pristine state, environmentally. Accordingly, we could say that the agency has, as a target, that the county will attain a state in which environmental quality will be maintained at high levels (which may be defined by the director in the form of governmental environmental quality standards). Development will occur only if it does not reduce the quality of the environment below certain levels. Second, the director appears to value either the extensive investigatory process for the master plan or its outcome; we cannot be sure of which. If the former is true, the second target for the agency is that it (the agency) engage in extensive, investigative activities that could contribute to the development of a master plan. In spite of substantial supporting evidence, we cannot be absolutely certain that the agency is approaching the targets that we identified. In fact, if political contingencies exist, it may be the case that the director will argue rather vigorously against our conclusions and affirm that other directions are the "real goals, targets, purposes, or whatever..." (regardless of our observations to the contrary).

There are two noteworthy aspects of these targets. First, note that the target focuses on a third and fourth order receiving system. The agency outputs recommendations only to the land-use commission (first order receiving system) that, in turn, outputs permits to builders (second order receiving systems) who, in turn, output buildings onto county building sites (third order receiving systems), which output various things to the ecological systems (air, soil, water) within the county. It is the state of these last systems that concerns the agency. In the second target, note that it focuses on a means or process for achieving an end. As we have said before, targets may focus on any aspect of the system, whereas goals should focus on the receiving system.

THE BEHAVIOR MANAGEMENT SPECIALIST AND SYSTEM GOALS AND VALUES

Your conceptual framework for systems should have grown considerably in this chapter. Although we only dealt with system goals and values, the ramifications of these two concepts are numerous. Let us summarize by weaving some aspects of goals and values through an example of a behavior management specialist working with a system within a large corporation.

Remember Lawrence Adams from Chapter One? He left Westronics Associates and joined a consultant firm that handled many organizational problems similar to those that Adams was trained to handle. A major project for Adams involved the evaluation and revision of an executive training and development (ETD) department within a large insurance firm. In the interest of brevity, we will dispense with the description of the system concepts discussed in Chapter Two and go directly to a consideration of ETD goals.

The director of ETD gave Adams a corporate report that listed the goals of ETD. They were: (1) to provide a forum for discussion of new and innovative management theories and strategies; (2) to provide training in four areas of executive development: employee relations, systematic planning, information utilization, and time management; and (3) to maintain a management resources center.

The director affirmed that these were the *aims* of ETD and that he "didn't believe in using the ambiguous term *goals*." (You surely have realized by now that it does not matter what you call them, but whatever you use for evaluation and control has to have the characteristics that we assign to *goals*.) Adams asked several questions to see if some other set of statements was available that could be goals even though ETD people called them something else. He found that each of the four executive development areas, employee relations, systematic planning, information utilization, and time management, had workshop or seminar *objectives*. Here is a sample:

- Managers should understand the difference between equal opportunity and affirmative action.
- To explore the various formats and uses of data-based decision making.
- To experience the "alternative matrix" approach to corporate planning.

With some sense of dismay, Adams began to seriously consider the conclusion that ETD did not have goals (by whatever name), as he knew them. ETD workshops inputted, processed, and outputted homogenous groups of managers and executives from various departments. There were no manifest statements that focused on the departments, nor was there any specific mention of the changed state of those departments or of the individual managers within departments. Adams began to look for the values that guided ETD.

By examining the processes carried out in the workshops and the outputs resulting, Adams identified a major terminal value that guided most of the decisions of the director of ETD. Bluntly stated, it was, "Managers and executives will express pleasure with their workshop experience and rate ETD efforts highly on postworkshop questionnaires."

Postworkshop questionnaires seemed to act as part of an informal feedback mechanism that the ETD director used to control the activities of ETD. It was significant to Adams that a workshop instructor had been moved to a different position when the questionnaire-based evaluation of his workshop had been interpreted as "a disturbing, thought-provoking experience that left participants with a number of questions about company policy." The workshop was also changed.

In addition, Adams began to detect some instrumental values having to do with multimedia presentations and "guest" speakers, but by this time he knew that before a behavior management approach could be implemented, there were several steps that should be taken. He recommended that: (1) a needs assessment be carried out for each of the departments that used the ETD, (2) goals (as we know them) be established, (3) alternatives to the usual workshop design (such as "behavioral rehearsal" and "reinforcement hierarchy identification") be considered to achieve the stated goals, and (4) feedback mechanisms appropriate to the goals be established.

Fortunately, the values of the system that we have identified as an insurance firm did not include maintenance of an operation such as ETD. Adams was able to present and defend his recommendations and a vice-president was put in charge of revamping ETD. Executive training and development is now a highly functional part of a well-designed management system encompassing the entire company.

It would be hard not to notice in this example that ETD as a system was connected to other systems and that subordinate-superordinate relationships existed (or should have existed). Several times in this chapter we have mentioned *receiving systems*, which suggests that systems do not exist in isolation. It is appropriate now for our discussion to turn to the interconnections between systems that we call networks. Chapter Four will introduce internal and external system networks and the many concepts associated with network analysis and design.

CHAPTER THREE:
GUIDELINES FOR PRACTICAL APPLICATION

Guideline 3.1: Before setting a behavior change program into operation, do what you can to determine whether or not goals exist for the system in which the behavior change is to occur.

—*You are looking for the four characteristics: focus on receiving system, specificity, time dimension, and manifest statements. To avoid confusion in your own mind about what a goal is, make it a very specific term. If the four characteristics are not there, it cannot be used for evaluation; therefore, it is not a goal.° Everything else is a target. Targets do not facilitate evaluation and control.*

—*You don't necessarily have to use the words and phrases used here to search out the characteristics of the system goals. (People in the system may not even see their stated directions, aims, purposes, and so forth, as "goals.") Develop a vocabulary and set of questions that are meaningful to individuals who may not be versed in the terminology of systems.*

—*When trying to determine system goals, be careful to avoid setting up a situation in which you are educating people in the system about what goals are. (This situation is much easier to produce than it may appear. After all, it makes sense to try to help them understand that for which you are looking.)*

—*Be careful to avoid inadvertently "creating" or setting goals for the system. (This also can be much easier than it may appear. Managers will be very grateful to you for helping them to "see" that their "goals" were really thus and such.)*

—*Eventually you may have to educate people in the system as to what goals are and help them formulate goals, but before you do it, make certain that they have accepted it as your new role (in addition to behavior change) or you may find resistance to the newly established goals during later stages.*

Guideline 3.2: *If the system does not have goals, look for the values that guide the system before you set a behavior change program into operation.*

—*Remember: system values (and, therefore, targets) may focus on anything from the physical appearance of the system to the number of employees; they may be vague and, most confusing of all, constantly changing; the dates or times when the values will be accomplished may be vague or changing; the values may be the property of management and may not be shared or recognized by others within the system.*

—*Remember: your values are not necessarily the system's values. If severe conflicts occur, you may have to choose between helping the system and*

°*"Goal" is an ambiguous term for most people. Using it in only this specific sense is not simply the petulant and pedantic whim of a behavior manager cum applied systems theorist, but rather a means of labeling those statements that can be used to facilitate evaluation from those that cannot.*

violating your own values (and perhaps ethics or integrity) or seeking employment elsewhere.

Guideline 3.3: *As you decide on which behaviors to change, look for conflicts between the proposed behavior change and the system goals or values.*

—*Regardless of how successful you are at changing behavior, the success will not be recognized if it does not contribute to the achievement of the system goals or targets (based on values).*

—*If the decider function is shared by a number of individuals and their values for the system differ, you may find that certain behavior changes will be supported by some decider members and not by others.*

—*If you have a number of behaviors to change, start with those that will contribute the most to the system goals or values.*

Guideline 3.4: *If you are evaluating a system, look for goals and values, just as you would for behavior changes. Make the identified goals or values the central focus of your evaluation.*

—*You want to be able to say, "Yes (or No), the system is (or is not) achieving whatever it is intended to achieve." However, beyond that, you should be able to judge the appropriateness of goals or values, given needs (see Chapter Seven); you should be able to assess the impact of goals (or lack thereof) on system functioning; and you should be able to recommend what needs to be done to have existing goals meet the requirements of the four characteristics or to convert values into appropriate goal statements.*

—*If the system that you are evaluating does not have goals, expect that system managers will believe that the system is functioning effectively; after all, their values have been guiding the system. However, this may not be the case if their management decisions are highly constrained by outside influences.*

Guideline 3.5: *When planning or designing a system, allot a major portion of your time for setting goals that conform to the four characteristics (see Chapter Eight).*

Guideline 3.6: *There are a number of goal setting procedures, but the most successful ones seem to have the following in common:*

—*Make it an iterative process; don't complete it in one meeting.*

—*Involve as many people as possible from all of the systems impacted by the goal-setting procedure.*

—*Stress the facilitative nature of goals for making systems revisions, not the win/lose, success/failure possibilities, based on judgments when using goals.*

Guideline 3.7: *Get used to viewing the decider function (management) as a subsystem that outputs to the system in question; thus, the decider will have goals that focus on the system while the system itself has goals that focus on its receiving systems.*

—*The goals of the decider function are often viewed as subgoals of the overall goal to be achieved. Don't fight with terminology; just keep in mind the relationships among decider, system, and receiving system and apply the characteristics of adequate goals. They function together nicely.*

FOUR
INTERNAL AND
EXTERNAL NETWORKS

PREVIEW GLOSSARY

Channel: a discrete path through a system or portion of a system, limited by its capacity to process signals. Examples: the official entrances into a national park are channels for inputs and outputs, and roads are channels for moving people through the park; the channels for inputs to an executive may be the telephone, mail, and personal contacts; if a regulatory agency systematically deals with all requests in one of four different ways, each of the four would be a channel.

Needs Assessment: a method for determining what inputs should be available to a receiving system in order for it to achieve desired states. Examples: a needs assessment for a program for the handicapped would determine what the program should input in order to achieve desired ends among the handicapped people that it services; a needs assessment for poverty-level families would find out what states the families should be in and would identify the inputs necessary to achieve those states.

As behavior managers increasingly see the systems and the highly complex interacting components within which behavior change takes place, they will need to develop means for conceptualizing and analyzing relationships within and among systems. Not only must current relationships be identified, but also those that will occur in newly evolving systems must be pinpointed. This is equally as true for physical or natural systems as it is for social or behavioral systems.

51

Ecological concerns have given rise to environmental impact analyses that are generally quite effective means for locating physical system interactions. Managers do not have similar "behavioral impact analysis" techniques for behavioral systems, but they will rapidly begin to see this need as behavioral technologies improve and system complexity is recognized. The intent of this chapter is to elaborate on some concepts that are evident in the behavioral system model and that are critical to the comprehension of complex system interactions. In addition, an outline of procedures to follow when pursuing an external network analysis is suggested, along with an example of a rather simplified network analysis. It should be noted from the outset that, although quantification in behavioral systems is possible and desirable, the emphasis in this chapter is on qualitative or conceptual aspects of behavioral system network analysis.

A premise basic to the following discussion is that networks are evident (and, indeed, planned) in social systems. These networks can be categorized as either internal or external. Internal networks exist within the boundaries of the system in question and are composed of various subsystem configurations. External networks consist of input-output relationships that the system in question has with other systems. Figure 4.1 illustrates diagramatically the arrangement of internal and external networks. Let us begin with a brief examination of internal networks and subsystems.

INTERNAL NETWORKS

As mentioned previously, internal networks are comprised of subsystems of the parent system. Each subunit of a major organization that carries out a separate function is a subsystem. You should note that subsystem analysis based on applied systems theory differs from organizational structure analysis in that subsystems are identified according to the processes that they carry out, whereas organizational or administrative analyses usually illustrate management hierarchies based on sub- and superordinate relationships. For instance, the Department of After-Care Services is a state-level bureaucratic or organizational entity that manages group homes for juvenile offenders and monitors juveniles on probation in their own homes or in foster homes. If one immediately accepts this entity as a system or subsystem, difficulty may ensue because the operation of the group homes is a part of the process of rehabilitation that cuts across bureaucratic lines and includes parts of the Institution for Juvenile Offenders, which, on an organizational chart, would be parallel with the

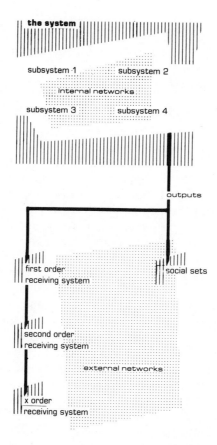

FIGURE 4.1 An illustration of a behavioral system with internal and external networks.

Department of After-Care Services. As one can see, the bureaucratic designation in this case does not coincide with the functional or subsystem breakdown.

System analysts are looking for sets of elements that interact to complete a process or function and they very well may find several within one administrative subdivision. The primary function of an internal network analysis is to identify subsystems that contribute to the total output of the system.

Subsystems

Subsystems can be classified according to the manner in which they relate to the system being considered. Although other authors (Miller, 1965a) have identified numerous subsystem types, a three-member classification scheme utilizing the terms *in-line, adjunct,* and *coupled* can be employed.

Most common is the *in-line subsystem,* which has a subordinate-superordinate relationship with the system or with other subsystems. As shown in Figure 4.2, in-line subsystems output to the system or to other subsystems but do not receive inputs from the system to which their outputs flow. They are arranged in a linear fashion so that inputs are processed and outputted to another system or subsystem. It can be seen that the relationship between subsystem A and subsystem B is a dependent one; that is, subsystem B is dependent upon subsystem A for inputs, but subsystem A hooks onto some other source for its inputs. Examples of this type of subsystem arrangement can be seen by the person caught up in the accounting web in a department store. When attempting to return merchandise, customers are often flowing through a series of in-line subsystems. The salesclerk sends the customer to the manager, who approves the return and sends the customer to the accounting department, where the return slip is signed, and then to the cashier, who finally hands the customer a cash refund.

Behavior management specialists have to anticipate subsystem arrangements in order to provide for efficient behavioral system operation. They also have to be aware that in-line subsystem configuration can result in bottlenecks that can cause considerable lost time "downstream" of the stoppage. Furthermore, the management of in-line subsystem configurations is much facilitated if all of the subsystems are controlled by the same manager. These precautionary decisions can be made during the planning stage if the system planner has identified that an in-line arrangement will exist.

Another type of subordinate-superordinate subsystem is the *adjunct subsystem.* The adjunct subsystem is different from the in-line subsystem in that it can receive inputs from the same system to which it outputs. As shown in Figure 4.3, the system has a prearranged linear flow with the adjunct subsystem situated tangentially. The system for one reason or another will output a signal to the adjunct subsystem, which will process the signal and output a new signal back to the system. Examples of such subsystems exist in organizations such as hospitals, where one goes from the emergency room to outpatient admitting and back to the emergency room, or from the doctor's office to the lab and back to the office. If one thinks of the patient as a signal (or as a signal carrying structure), in a case such as the emergency room, the signal cannot be processed until it is

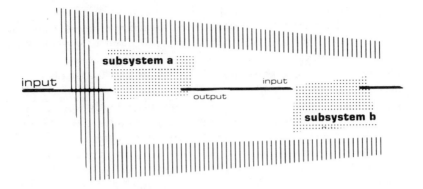

FIGURE 4.2   An in-line subsystem configuration.

changed in some manner by the outpatient admitting adjunct subsystem and returned.

Because adjunct subsystems are not a part of the main-line, linear flow, the step in the process prior to the adjunct subsystem is usually a decision or branching point. In various forms, the question asked is generally, "Does a certain condition exist?" If yes, then one direction is taken—perhaps to the adjunct subsystem. If the answer is no, then another path or channel is followed.

A problem that behavior managers must recognize and anticipate when encountering or formulating adjunct subsystem arrangements is that the adjunct subsystem usually will not be a part of the system in question. This generally means that the adjunct subsystem is managed by indi-

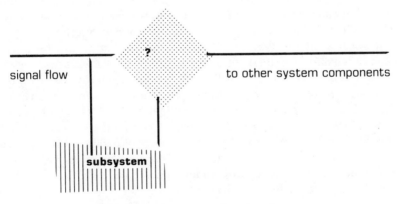

FIGURE 4.3   An adjunct subsystem.

viduals other than those managing the subsystems in the original flow. This can result in excessive delays or inadequate work if contingencies on the adjunct subsystem place high priorities on connections to systems other than the one in question. As the number of adjunct subsystems increases, the amount of control over system operations decreases. Given various requirements of the system, this condition may be one that could be troublesome for behavior managers. They would certainly work to avoid such a condition if influence could be exercised during the planning stages. If you remember the situation of Adams and Westronics in Chapter One, the problem there was that the plan developers relied upon an engineering group that was an adjunct subsystem. Behavior management techniques could not be successful in an arrangement where outside forces kept the behavior from occurring.

Berrien (1968) identified another type of system-subsystem relationship, which he described as *coupled*. This structure occurs when an interdependent flow of inputs and outputs exists, as shown in Figure 4.4. A dyad is formed when system A of the pair is dependent upon system B for its inputs, while system B is also dependent upon system A for its inputs. Should either of the systems cease to output to the other system, both systems would be forced into different behaviors or inactivity because of lack of inputs.

The plant-animal expiration-respiration cycle is often given as an example of a coupled system relationship. In social systems, any unit such as a laboratory, which receives its inputs from another unit, for instance, a diagnostic clinic, which in turn is dependent upon the lab, is, in part, characteristic of the coupled system arrangement. The problem for behavior management specialists is to determine the extent to which the two systems or subsystems are actually interdependent. Casual observation of social systems suggests that the degree of interdependency is usually less than 100 percent. Most social systems have multiple input sources that can replace each other and continue the flow of inputs to the system for processing and output back to the original system.

Regardless of the type, every behavioral subsystem can be further broken down and described according to the process taking place within that subsystem. Processes, you will recall, are the means by which outputs are produced. In behavioral systems, processes are primarily chains of behavior performed either by an individual or by a group of persons prepared to work in a purposeful sequence. A thorough discussion of these processes or *behavioral subsystems* is the focus of Chapter Five, but one should presently keep in mind that any proposed system with human components in subsystems will undoubtedly have behavioral requirements that can be analyzed and specified.

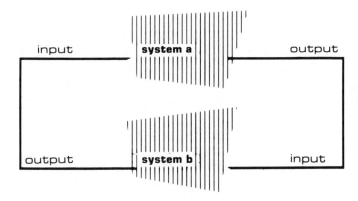

FIGURE 4.4   A coupled systems configuration.

Over the years the utilization of systems theory as a means for understanding social or physical relationships has been characterized by an emphasis on subsystem or internal network identification. External networks are equally important but oftentimes more difficult to perceive than internal networks. However, a grasp of the relevant concepts should permit behavior management specialists to work as comfortably with external as with internal networks.

EXTERNAL NETWORKS

A primary aspect of understanding external networks in behavioral systems is the identification of *receiving systems*. As shown in Figure 4.1, a receiving system for any system is the organization to which outputs flow. Stated another way, the receiving system takes in as inputs the specific outputs of some other designated system. Receiving system is not a common term in systems literature, although the concept occurs and the need exists for a descriptive label (Brethower, 1972). It is not uncommon to see the receiving system referred to as *suprasystem* despite the fact that the latter nomenclature has been specifically applied to a distinctly different concept.

Receiving Systems and Suprasystems

Whereas the *suprasystem* for any given system is the larger unit in the hierarchical arrangement, the receiving system need not even be an obvious part of that arrangement. The reverse is also true; whereas the receiving system's inputs comes from the system in question, the suprasystem need not receive any inputs from that same system. To further confuse the issue, since supra- and receiving systems are not mutually exclusive concepts, a suprasystem could receive inputs from one of its subsystems and therefore be both a supra- and a receiving system. A concrete instance of this situation exists in most industries where the personnel department outputs recommendations for management hiring to upper level division managers. The personnel department would be a subsystem of one of those upper level divisions; hence, that division is both the suprasystem and the receiving system. From the preceding example, it is apparent that a distinction should be made between suprasystem and receiving system. Furthermore, it is often useful to discriminate the *goal-related receiving system* from the *target-related receiving system*.

Goal-related and Target-related Receiving Systems

If one identifies the goals for a specific system, it follows, according to the definition of goals in Chapter Three, that a receiving system will also be identified. For example, suppose the system in question is a pathology laboratory that studies cell tissues at the request of a cancer treatment center: its goal is to provide decisive information for the center on 98 percent of the requests within 2 hours of the time the request is made. Given such a goal, it is automatically established that the cancer treatment center is the receiving system of the pathology laboratory. The outputs of the pathology lab flow to the cancer treatment center and become the inputs for that particular system. Because the goal of the lab relates to those outputs moving to the treatment center, the center is the *goal-related* receiving system.

The pathology laboratory could have other receiving systems, however, that do not coincide with established goals. Consider the case in which copies of the reports from the laboratory go to a research center as well as to the treatment center. If no goal has been stated that necessitates the flow of certain outputs (reports) to specific locations (receiving systems), yet that output flow exists, it must be concluded that a *target* has evolved for the lab and the exact nature of that target will have to be inferred from the quality and quantity of the outputs from the laboratory, which become inputs for the research center. The research center is clearly a receiving system for the lab and since the arrangement was not part of the goal of the lab, the research center must be labeled as a *target-related* receiving system.

The Special Case of Being Output and Receiving System

Viewing receiving systems as either target- or goal-related is one way of discerning input-output interrelationships, but behavior managers using a systems perspective will quickly discover that other more confusing arrangements often exist. In many cases of behavioral systems, the signal being processed is one of deficit behavior, that is, the specified output of the system is an individual whose behavior repertoire is increased over what it was when the system was entered. Most instructional systems are, in fact, of this nature. The output of such a system is often stated as, "individuals with X ... Y ... Z ... behaviors" or in the behavioral objective style, "The student can (or will be able to) do X ... Y ... Z ..., given A ... B ... C ...." The newly acquired behaviors listed as system outputs are often designed for use by the individual rather than for some other social group. This means that the individual passing through the system is both output and receiving system. An example of such a situation is one in which a system (school or classroom) outputs individuals with decision-making behaviors to be used with personal problems. If the individual enters the system without specific decision-making behaviors but learns them in the system, that person is both the output of the decision-making behavior training system and the system that uses the decision-making behaviors. Of course, not all training systems must demonstrate this condition.

For example, suppose the decision-making behaviors taught in the training system described above dealt with industrial development rather than with individual problems. The training system would still output a person with decision-making skills, but in this case, the industry employing the person and using the skills would be the receiving system.

Second Order Receiving Systems

If one begins to consider needs assessment based on external network arrangements, it quickly becomes apparent that more than just the initial receiving system is important for a clear grasp of behavioral system functioning. One needs to look beyond the first receiving system to understand the total flow and impact that an output from one system will have on subsequent systems. For example, suppose that a behavior management specialist, along with other professionals, is trying to deal with the problems of the elderly and proposes the establishment of a Bureau for the Aged (BFA) that, among other things, will output information about nutritional diets for persons over 70 years of age. Is it sufficient to simply identify the flow of outputs (dietary information) from the Bureau to the regional offices (first order receiving systems)? Might it not also be beneficial to extend the analysis of the network to second and third order receiving systems? The answer is affirmative because such network analysis allows the planning group to see what other systems will have to be dealt with and what contingencies will have to be considered. In the case of the Bureau for the Aged proposal, the network analysis may very well result in the arrangement that appears in Figure 4.5. From that network diagram, one can see that the ultimate users of the information are actually second and third order receiving systems. The proposed plan has to account for the flow of information through the intervening first and second order receiving systems and for ultimate utilization of the information by those who provide food services for the elderly.

In this example, the network ends with the receiving system that uses the information to output a product that is not information but physical substances. The existence of those substances as outputs is to some degree dependent upon the input of information. The network flow is linear and has a clear terminal point.

Yet another arrangement found in social systems is the case in which the system receives its own outputs and, ergo, is its own receiving system. We are not referring to components of a system (No. 1) also belonging to another system (No. 2) and, while functioning for System No. 2, receiving outputs from System No. 1. A much more direct input-output flow is suggested here. As an example, consider a family as a system. It outputs shelter in the form of a house or apartment, and provides protection for the family. The same system that is outputting the shelter is also receiving the protection by using the shelter. There is no other system for which the system (family) is providing the shelter. If a family rents its home to another family, it must still seek out shelter, which it provides for itself. Communities output fire and police services to the members of the community, that is, to themselves. The planet earth, as a social system, must be considered this type of receiving system for its own outputs until a satellite, a moon colony, or some other receiving system is created. There are a number of evaluation-oriented groups that output the standards to be used as criteria for evaluation and then use those standards to evaluate something else (or even themselves).

Lest the reader interpret the above comments as critical of such a situation, let us clarify the problem. To the extent that a system is its own receiving system, it meets only its own need states. It must, in a sense, step outside itself in order to have information that will allow for regulation of itself. Hence, most systems that are their own receiving systems have limited external feedback; they may output whatever meets their self-established output specifications. This may or may not be detrimental to

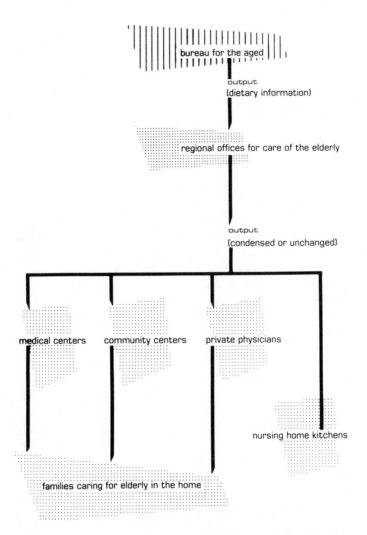

FIGURE 4.5   An illustration of an external network.

the functioning of the system. The erudite professor who lectures on and on to a sleeping class and thoroughly enjoys himself is not functioning adequately if changes in student behavior are an intended output of the class. On the other hand, the community that is constantly looking to other communities for models of development may benefit from an increase in self-identified standards.

Social Sets

Our discussion to this point has centered on *systems* that receive outputs, but the reader should be aware that sets of receiving systems will sometimes receive inputs individually and, in fact, not go together to form a larger system. To classify any arrangement of components as a system, one needs to establish interrelationships and interactions among parts. If the elements that receive outputs from a particular system can be easily grouped but show no evidence of relationship or interaction to form a larger whole, that group should be called a *social set*. Given this designation, one recognizes that individual members of the set receive inputs and have some characteristic in common with other set members and that the output from a social set is simply the cumulative total output of the members of the set. Consider, for example, the Census Bureau outputting population data to registered urban planners. Regarded collectively, the planners are a social set rather than a system unless they interact and, thereby, form a larger unit that is, in some sense, greater than just the sum of its parts. In the network analysis of the Census Bureau, the behavior management specialist will have to identify urban planners as a set of individuals receiving information from the Bureau rather than as a receiving system that will act upon the inputs in some coordinated fashion.

Summary

To summarize, behavioral systems produce outputs that flow to other systems or social sets and become inputs for those systems or sets. The term *receiving system* has been coined to specify that system to which outputs flow. Receiving systems can be further identified as first order, second order, and so on, according to their placement "downstream" of the original system. A variety of receiving system arrangements are possible, and the behavior management specialist should anticipate anything from multiple branches to returning loops.

Having established a conceptual framework for internal and external network analyses, let us go on to an example of analysis of an existing system.

AN EXAMPLE OF EXTERNAL
AND INTERNAL NETWORKS

An example of a portion of the results of an external network analysis is illustrated in Figure 4.6. The original system was a research grant foundation that was contemplating significant changes in its focus and operation. A behavior management specialist was engaged to assist in the

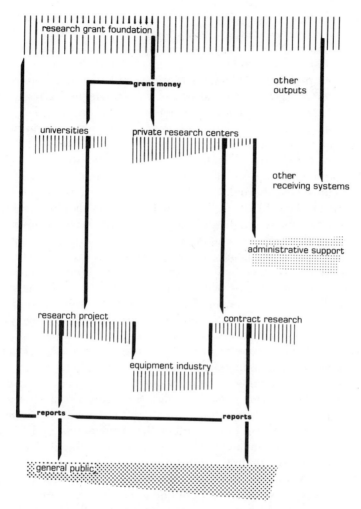

FIGURE 4.6   Example of an external network
analysis.

changes because the directors of the foundation believed that it could
better utilize the experts it retained to evaluate proposals and influence
the type of research that it sponsored. Before planning or designing any
changes, the behavior management specialist analyzed both the internal
and external networks. The external network analysis revealed that five
major classes of outputs were produced: research reports, proposal specifications, grant money, public relations information, and accounting
information. These outputs went to five different first order receiving

systems although some systems received more than one output. By pursuing the original outputs from the research foundation through several second and third order receiving systems, the behavior management specialist was able to identify several substantially different outputs that were not part of the original output ensemble but that were directly related. In some cases, these input/output flows proceeded as far as fourth order receiving systems before the network was terminated. The two predominant terminal situations were systems outputting inquiries, applications, or reports back to the research foundation and systems whose outputs were not clearly affected by the inputs in question.

Having knowledge of this network configuration, the behavior management specialist could firmly disagree with a professor on the proposal review board who suggested that incentives should be set up for universities to submit grant applications. The professor believed that, "they (universities) are the only organizations we service, anyway." At a later time, the behavior management specialist was again able to utilize her knowledge of the external network. She pointed out to the board of directors that questionnaires sent to only the first order receiving systems were not likely to provide much information because the important information would come from second and third order receiving systems, and they were not likely to return questionnaires. One obvious reason that they would not return questionnaires as first order systems had done in the past was that the foundation had no implicit (or explicit) contingencies in their behavior, as it did with the first order systems that received grants.

Whereas the external network analysis in Figure 4.6 illustrates what happens beyond the research foundation's output boundary, the internal network analysis in Figure 4.7 identifies the arrangement of subsystems within the system boundaries. The research grant foundation is "the system"; its supra- or parent system in a hierarchical arrangement is a philanthropic foundation that has within its boundaries a social program foundation as well as the research foundation. Five parallel subsystems exist within the research grant foundation; each of these subsystems is independent from all the others and carries out a specific function. Three subsystems have an adjunct subsystem to which they send requests for printing and from which they receive printed reports, announcements, and so forth. The research grant foundation has a rather straightforward subsystem arrangement that is not difficult to recognize. Larger bureaucratic structures often present highly complex situations with interlocking and overlapping configurations that make diagrammatic representation difficult, if not impossible.

Since subsystems can be further subdivided, a simple description of subsystems is not a complete internal network analysis. *Process* analyses of each subsystem reveal the behavioral sequences that are followed to

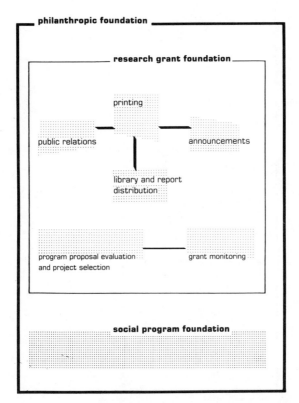

FIGURE 4.7 An example of internal network analysis in a behavioral system.

convert the input to output. Figure 4.8 is an example of a flowchart representation of the process employed in the proposal evaluation and project selection subsystem. It is presented here only as an illustration of the results of process or *behavioral subsystem* analysis. The logic and procedures behind the analysis of subsystem process is sufficiently lengthy to merit an entire chapter (see Chapter Five). You must keep in mind, nonetheless, that changes in almost any aspect of a system can result in changes in the behavioral subsystem and possible changes in output that could have ramifications throughout the entire external network.

Having completed both internal and external network analyses for an existing system or for a proposed new system, the behavior management specialist is in a good position to anticipate problems and to prepare preventive measures. To a certain extent, techniques to do this have already been developed with natural systems and will be impacted by new

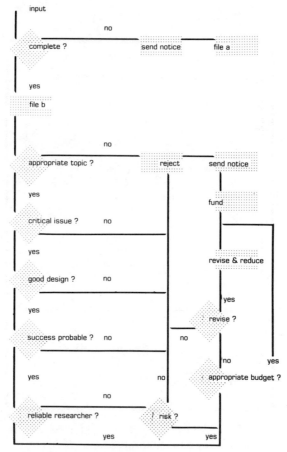

FIGURE 4.8   An example of process or behavioral subsystem analysis.

or revised sociotechnical systems controlled by humans. This can and should now also be done for behavioral systems.

CHAPTER FOUR:
GUIDELINES FOR PRACTICAL APPLICATION

Guideline 4.1: Use the following five steps to do an external network analysis: (1) identify outputs from the system, (2) identify receiving systems, (3) follow original output through each receiving system, (4) identify next order receiving systems, and (5) repeat steps 3 and 4 until the output is no longer related to the original output.

Step 1 is probably the most difficult. There are five major sources of information about system outputs. They are the system designer/planner, the receiving systems, the decider, the process components, and whoever handles inputs and outputs as they cross the respective boundaries, such as secretaries, mail clerks, and shipping room personnel.

—Remember: In relation to Step 1, the individuals performing the decider function can provide information to you about the projected type and rate of outputs related to the goals that the system is attempting to meet. In addition, the decider can often identify those unintentional outputs that are highly visible. Less noticeable outputs are sometimes recognized by the persons who handle them last in the system but often can only be detected by your systematic observation of the system.

—Remember: A situation sometimes exists where outputs will leave the system before having gone completely through the entire process. For this reason, the behavior manager should consult with process components to identify these "in-process" outputs. The receiving systems and especially those people who handle inputs of receiving systems can often provide information about system outputs (receiving system inputs) that are not readily identified by members of the original outputting system. Finally, the designer(s)/planner(s) of the system may be able to pinpoint outputs that occur one time only, on an intermittent but regular schedule, or as irregular, unpredictable events.

—Keep in mind that, once the output ensemble has been established (Step 1), you must determine the receiving system to which each output flows (Step 2). The receiving system will process the input and produce outputs relevant to or dependent upon the original input. Those receiving system outputs not related to inputs from the original system are ignored. Those that are highly relevant to the original system's output are followed to the second order receiving system, where the same evaluation of input/output relationship is made. This procedure is repeated until a receiving system: (1) does not output anything related to the original input, (2) is minimally affected by the input, that is, its outputs do not change appreciably whether the input is there or not, (3) is a receiving system for its own outputs, or (4) outputs back to the original system.

In each case, the external network is terminated. This procedure is followed for each output from the original system.

Guideline 4.2: *If you are called upon to change behaviors of individuals employed within a system, make certain that their jobs and the intended outcomes of their jobs are clearly defined before taking any action.*

—*You may find that a system has two or more subsystems operating to achieve quite different ends. Further, what appears to be a behavior management problem may simply be a case of individuals being asked to slip back and forth from subsystem to subsystem without knowing that different jobs are related to different purposes and outcomes. You can help by recognizing and clarifying which tasks are to be done when and for what purposes.*

—*You will find that, any time subsystems share a component, there will be conflicts and performance problems unless all of the system employees involved understand their dual roles.*

Guideline 4.3: If, while looking at internal and external networks of a system, you find that much of what a system does is for its own use, suspect that the system has become its own receiving system and that it may be operating for its own ease or self-preservation.

This poses a difficult problem for you if behavior change is your goal. System members will resist a change that increases their work load or eliminates situations that perhaps were not functional but were obviously positively reinforcing.

FIVE
BEHAVIORAL SUBSYSTEMS

The purpose of Chapter Five is to elaborate on the concept of internal networks that was introduced in Chapter Four. This discussion will be based upon the proposition that many social systems have within them human components whose major contribution to systems can best be described as functioning *behavioral subsystems. Behavioral systems* had previously been defined as those systems that had within them a behavioral sequence or component carried out by humans. Behavioral *sub*systems are those sequences or components within systems that involve human behavior. Miller (1965b) implicitly included this subsystem under system processes, that is, whatever happens between input and output boundaries of living systems to change matter, energy, or information is process, and an apparent aspect of process in social systems is action or behavior. Therefore, in order to understand process in many social systems, a behavioral perspective is necessary. The behavior management specialist who utilizes a systems orientation to understand the context in which behavior occurs either accounts for the impact that changes will have on the environment and behavior of organisms within systems or runs the risk of facing unexpected and perhaps undesirable effects. Because behavioral sequences within social systems are inextricably connected to other systems through input-output channels (external networks), the individual who must design, manage, or change a social system should be aware of the behavioral interdependency of one social system upon another.

If one cannot observe the behavioral aspects within a subsystem, the "black-box" situation is generally proposed (Ashby, 1958; Beishon, 1971). This simply is a means for saying that the system exists and that its inputs and outputs are identifiable, but that we cannot determine what is occurring between the input and output boundaries. The black box designation is unusual in the analysis or synthesis of behavioral systems. It is generally possible to identify the actions taken and the decisions made in behavioral systems, as opposed to natural systems. This is not to say that it is always easy. For example, the task of tracing an input through the maze of a social welfare agency with its myriad of alternate channels, given various conditions, can be a major headache, but it is not impossible.

The remainder of this chapter is devoted to an explanation of behavioral subsystems and a consideration of the problems of structural description, conflicting terminology, analysis approach, and possible control techniques. Let us start with a few brief definitions for important terms.

PREVIEW GLOSSARY

Contingencies: if/then relationships existing between behaviors and consequences. Examples: if the administrative assistant always has memos on the administrator's desk on time, then that person will not be criticized for late work; this is a contingency that could exist in an office. A contingency for a small business development program might be: if the proposal outline is completed accurately, then program officials will help the client locate financial support.

Reinforcing Stimuli: consequences that follow a behavior and increase or decrease the frequency of subsequent occurrences of that behavior. Pleasant consequences tend to increase the behavior that they follow, while aversive consequences tend to decrease the behavior that they follow. The loss of an order was an aversive consequence (reinforcing stimulus) that decreased the salesman's behavior of using the client's nickname without invitation to do so; praise from a superior was a pleasant consequence that increased the behavior of proper tool use on the part of a road gang laborer.

Discriminative Stimuli: things in the environment that one has learned to recognize as signals for certain consequences. Examples: rising (feeding) trout are a signal (discriminative stimulus) that a hooked fish should occur (pleasant consequence) if an artificial fly is laid appropriately upon the water; a client's nod of agreement is a signal that, if offered the contract now, he will sign and accept the proposed terms; a malfunctioning gauge is a signal that the operation should be stopped before loss of coolant occurs.

BEHAVIORAL SUBSYSTEM STRUCTURE

Behavioral subsystems in behavioral systems are characterized by sequences of actions carried out by the organisms that comprise a portion of the system. The actions of such organisms can fulfill any of the functions that Miller (1965b&c) attributes to system components, but they, nonetheless, perform actions that are often predictable, observable, and essential to system functioning. These behavioral subsystems need not be regarded as enclosed in a "black box." The techniques of applied behavioral analysis are appropriate for analysis of behavioral subsystems (Baer et al., 1968; Ferster et al., 1975; Millenson, 1967). Other behaviorally oriented approaches such as flowcharting are also applicable to the identification of such subsystems; more will be said about this later. First, however, let us examine several situations and develop the idea that behavioral subsystems are an integral aspect of the internal network of social systems.

Consider a group of farmers living in a river basin much like the Egyptians dwelling in the Nile River Valley prior to the construction of the Aswan Dam. According to Jones's (1967, pp. 1–11) system taxonomy, this agriculturally based civilization would be made up of administrative and voluntary systems linked primarily with environmental, biological, and physical systems. Careful observation of the human operatives within this group would reveal that certain highly differentiated behaviors occur in a specific sequence and that those behaviors not only are preceded by actions of a physical system, the river, but are also precipitated by actions of the river. In the spring the river receives runoff water and soil from its tributaries at a greater input rate than its normal boundaries can maintain and, as a result, its banks are overcome and the land is covered with silt-carrying water. When the water recedes, nutrient-rich soil remains over great stretches of the river valley. In system terms, it could be said that the river system outputs the water and soil to the environmental and administrative system, of which the primitive farmers are a part. The water and soil input is changed at the input boundary of the agricultural system to a signal, indicating the initiation of a behavior chain that progresses to the ultimate end—the output of foodstuffs.

From the viewpoint of the behavior analyst (and hopefully the planner who may disrupt the system), each defined behavior of the human operatives (such as seeding) is chained to the preceding behavior (such as plowing). Each behavior is maintained in the sequence by the stimuli that follow it and act as conditioned reinforcers. An input from another system initiates the chain, and discriminative and reinforcing stimuli perpetuate the flow. Each behavior is preceded by a condition or stimulus that signals that the behavior should occur and is followed by a condition or stimulus that reinforces the occurrence of the behavior that preceded it. Removal or alteration of either type of stimuli could disrupt the entire chain.

In another instance a hospital emergency room illustrates a case in which several different, parallel behavioral subsystems function, depending upon the input. The system boundary has few restrictive conditions as long as the input is human. However, the stimuli arising from the person handling inputs (nurse, receptionist) signal different behavioral chains on the part of emergency room staff, depending upon such circumstances as whether or not the patient's life is threatened. Given differential inputs, the behaviors of people within the system follow well-defined, discriminably different sequences that result in various outcomes, ranging in this case from deceased to well patients. Appropriate actions on the part of the individuals in both the agricultural and the medical emergency system are an integral aspect of system functioning and, therefore, are an essential consideration whenever a behavioral system is being proposed or evaluated.

Behavioral subsystems need not be restricted to groups of human beings, as the two previous examples would suggest. Frisch's (1974) work with honey bees is an excellent illustration of "natural" or animal-social systems with well-defined behavioral subsystems. The interaction of scout bees with plant systems initiates a sequence of discrete, highly differentiated behaviors that, in turn, serve as stimuli for specific behaviors on the part of forager bees. The chain of behaviors from "scouting" to "exploration of blossoms" to "return to hive" to "prescribed dancelike movements" to "nectar collection" to "return to hive" form a sequence that is dependent upon inputs from other subsystems and that is essential to the production of outputs, such as honey from the system, that is, the hive. As the fruit farmer-honey producer well knows, thoughtless intervention in the system network can result in behavioral changes that will influence the outputs of more than one system. In fact, it is the behavior of the bees that connects the "hive system" to the "orchard system" and produces fruit and honey.

If the foregoing instances are valid examples of behavioral subsystems within social systems, it can be argued that other social systems would also have such subsystems. Moreover, because of the relationships that must exist for open systems, it can be argued that many behavioral subsystems will be dependent upon inputs from other systems that are not necessarily a part of the hierarchy but rather, perhaps, only part of the total network of systems.

Given the assumed existence of behavioral subsystems and the possible relationship that they may have to other systems, it might be well to distinguish between behaviors as process in subsystems and behaviors as outputs of systems.

BEHAVIORAL SUBSYSTEMS
VERSUS BEHAVIORS AS OUTPUTS

A conceptual problem arises if individual humans are considered to be behavioral systems. Some treatments of human psychology refer to specific behaviors on the part of individuals as outputs from a system, not as system process, as put forth presently. A possible resolution of this apparent conflict might be signaled by the work of several applied behavioral system studies in which behavioral products, and not behaviors, were evaluated in the same manner that behaviors are often considered in other behavioral analysis studies. For instance, Kohlenberg et al. (1976) dealt with families or households as systems that outputted the products of behavior patterns carried out within the system. Specifically, Kohlenberg and his associates evaluated kilowatt-hour consumption, which is obviously the result or product of certain behaviors rather than a behavior itself. The authors did not observe or attempt to change within-system behaviors directly, but rather, only measured a specific output of the system. It was assumed that individual behaviors would change when contingencies impinging on the system changed and that concomitant change in system output would result.

An approach of this type requires a differentiation between *intrasystem* contingencies and *intersystem* contingencies. Intrasystem contingencies operate within a behavioral system and exist between the executive component of the system (decider) and individuals who are components of the behavioral subsystem. If the component behaves in ways appropriate to the process necessary for a specific output, certain positive consequences will arise from the decider or a designated surrogate. This type of contingency is exemplified quite clearly in token economy studies (Doleys et al., 1981; Kazdin, 1975; Kazdin & Geesey, 1980; Robinson et al., 1981; Winkler, 1971) wherein individuals within the system perform in a prescribed manner to earn tokens.

Intersystem contingencies also exist between the decider of a behavioral system and some system in the environment. If the system outputs the appropriate products at acceptable rates, the effect on the environment will be such that certain consequences will arise from the environment and be available to the system. A number of authors (Kohlenberg et al., 1976; Slavin et al., 1981; Winett et al., 1977; Winett et al., 1979) have demonstrated this type of contingency existing between a utility company and families. The electric company, as part of the family system's environment, could not place contingencies upon individual members of the family, but it could place contingencies upon the family or residence as a system and assume that, through the decider's manipulation of intrasystem contingencies, the behavioral subsystem would change. Appropriate changes in the behavioral subsystem would result in changes in the products outputted from the system. Behavioral products become the significant measure when outputs of behavioral subsystems are of prime importance.

Thus, humans are viewed as outputting behavior when considered individually but, when considered as part of a behavioral system, the behaviors of individuals become part of the system process, and the *products* of the behaviors viewed collectively become the outputs. This distinction between behaviors outputted from individuals within systems and products outputted from systems as a result of behavioral subsystem functioning is an important one for the behavior management specialist to keep in mind while planning or managing social systems. The behavior manager who recognizes that the behavior of an individual is essential to the overall process of a system has already established the part-whole relationship between individual and system. The manager who identifies the cues and contingencies existing and necessary for the occurrence of individual behaviors and, hence, adequate system functioning has significantly increased the likelihood of the proposed system achieving the goals for which it was established.

BEHAVIORAL SUBSYSTEM ANALYSIS

The behavior manager considering behavioral subsystems as part of social systems has at least two analytical approaches to employ.

The techniques of applied behavior analysis with which the behavior manager is already familiar have been mentioned several times above although another approach, called *flowcharting* is available. Flowcharting grew out of computer system analysis and design techniques but has a derived counterpart applicable to human behavior (Morasky, 1980; Page et al., 1976). Figure 5.1 is an example of flowcharting applied to one of the behavioral subsystems existing in an estate planning company. In its simplest form, flowcharting uses rectangles to indicate actions taken in a process and diamonds to indicate decision points. Decisions are usually reduced to binary choices, that is, "yes" or "no," but such a condition is not absolutely necessary. Decision points or diamonds often result in two separate paths, one of which is the main track, and the other is usually a corrective alternative that may return to the main track behind or forward of the point at which it originated.

Flowcharting is a straightforward means for graphically presenting sequences of behavior, but it does not account for the signals or contingencies that influence the actual occurrence of the behavior.

On the other hand, the behavioral principles approach that utilizes

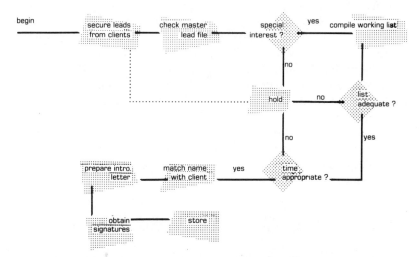

FIGURE 5.1   Flowchart from an estate planning firm
depicting client reference system.

techniques of operant psychology and applied behavior analysis does
concentrate on the identification of contingencies on behavior. The
identification of discriminative stimuli, behaviors, and reinforcing stimuli
that go together to form chains is essentially an identification of contingencies operating within systems. Discriminative stimuli (S^D) are generally viewed as stimuli signaling that reinforcement will occur if certain
behaviors are performed. Reinforcing stimuli (S^R) are those stimuli that
give rise to an increase in a particular behavior when they occur immediately after the occurrence of that behavior. It is generally believed by
operant psychologists that stimuli are discriminative and reinforcing at the
same time when in behavior chains; thus, a certain amount of stimulus
control over behaviors exists in behavior chains, that is, certain behaviors
will not be reinforced unless specific contingencies are in effect. Various
stimuli take on discriminative properties because they signal the presence
of contingencies; hence, entire chains of behavior that are integral aspects
of system functioning are dependent upon certain stimuli and contingencies. The techniques of applied behavior analysis were designed to
reveal those stimuli and contingencies as well as the effect that they have
on behaviors.

It has been demonstrated many times over in studies appearing in
behavior analysis journals that certain changes in contingencies will result
in predictable changes in behavior. It has also been suggested that
inability to produce behavior change often results from lack of power or

authority to control system contingencies existing at higher levels or arising from higher echelons (Ross & Price, 1976). If the output of specific behavioral products from behavioral systems is dependent upon the operation of discrete behavior chains or behavior subsystems and the operation of those systems is dependent upon specific discriminative and reinforcing stimuli, it would seem that the understanding and planning of social systems would include the understanding of behavioral subsystems. Hence, it seems that the comprehensive planner/system analyst could use the techniques of the applied behavior analyst and vice versa. It may be that a multidisciplinary planning team is necessary in order to provide for the consideration of the extensive number of factors that have to be taken into account.

CONTROL OF BEHAVIORAL SUBSYSTEMS

For those concerned with social planning and control or management, a question arises as to the most effective method for changing behavioral subsystems. Can behavioral subsystems and, hence, social systems be changed only by inputting new contingencies? Posed another way: if one were to design a System A, which had as a goal the modification of the behavioral subsystem or the behavioral products outputted from System B, would contingencies be the only goal-oriented output of System A to System B? Research on energy conservation (Cone & Hayes, 1980; Kohlenberg et al, 1976; Seaver & Vernon, 1976), paper recycling (Witmer & Geller, 1976), and littering (Bacon-Pure, et al., 1980; Kohlenberg & Phillips, 1973; O'Neill et al., 1980) suggests that the answer is "yes"; however, other work (Hayes & Cone, 1977, 1981; Leitenberg et al., 1968) strongly suggests that if System A simply provides a feedback mechanism, which gives information about the output of System B, for System B, System B will change its behavioral subsystem and effect a change in output. This assumes, however, that System B, once apprised of its output type and rates, perceives a change as desirable, that is, the feedback mechanism provides information indicating an output rate outside of desirable levels.

It would seem that behavioral subsystems also must change when necessary inputs cease or are substantially altered in some way. The construction of an upstream dam that prevents spring flooding will influence the behavioral subsystems of primitive farmers downstream who depend upon the new soil and water inputted with the spring floods. A similar situation occurs when a labor strike halts the flow of materials from a materials preparation plant to the assembly site (plant). The contingencies impinging upon the human components in either of the systems examples above remain the same; it is only the critical discriminative stimuli that are missing. That is, the if-then relationship of behavior to reinforcement has not changed, but the discriminative stimuli that signal that reinforcement will occur are missing. Hence, the behavioral subsystem changes.

There are also circumstances where *controlled* change of behavioral subsystems is not deemed appropriate; in those cases, it appears that information pertaining to long-range consequences is often outputted from one system to another, *hoping* that behavioral subsystem change will occur. Consider, for example, the groups in the Western world whose express aim is to reduce the rate of increase of the population. To do this the behavioral subsystems of many social systems will need to change, but no one agency yet has the power to impose the necessary contingencies to force change. Therefore, natural, long-range contingencies are publicized, and the people within the systems may change behaviors or not as they so choose, or as other contingencies may dictate.

AN EXAMPLE OF
BEHAVIORAL SUBSYSTEM PLANNING

Many profit-making companies or organizations are essentially behavioral systems whose major output or product may be tangible or nontangible. When planning for substantial changes, managers can anticipate the formation of new behavioral subsystems or the disruption of satisfactorily functioning ones. A concrete example from an estate planning firm may help to illustrate how planning can include consideration of behavioral subsystems.

Atlantic Associates was a highly successful estate planning organization whose management was exploring the possibility of expanding the operation to include an entirely new service, which, of course, would necessitate a new behavioral subsystem. Since Atlantic was a small, highly specialized firm, new personnel were to be added only after thorough analysis of present skills and future needs. Market analysis, goal setting, and other aspects of the proposed expansion were undertaken. Further, however, the behavioral subsystems already in operation were identified and detailed. Figure 5.2 illustrates in flowchart fashion one major behavioral system that involved several key employees. Steps 7, 9, and 10, in particular, necessitated the skills of one individual. Since this individual worked on a commission basis, the financial contingencies associated with completing these steps were apparent. Also apparent to the behavior analyst were the signals arising from Steps 6, 8, and 9, which indicated that subsequent steps should be initiated. Thus, the discriminative stimuli

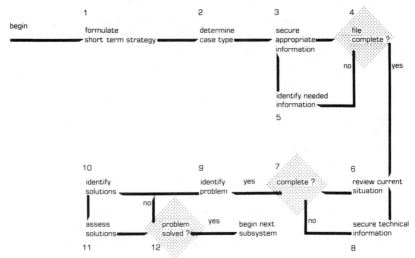

FIGURE 5.2   Flowchart of plan development procedure in an estate planning firm.

signaling the behavior, the behavior itself, and at least one possible
reinforcer had been identified.

By identifying the behavioral subsystems associated with the proposed new service, it was discovered that the same individual who was
critical to Steps 7, 9, and 10 in Figure 5.2 would also be critical to several
steps in the newly planned subsystem. Time would not permit the
completion of all steps in both subsystems by one person without predictable delays. Delays are often necessary and tolerable but would that be
the only disruption to present systems? Continued analysis of contingencies revealed that, although commissions were roughly equivalent, the
individual critical to Steps 7, 9, and 10 would probably spend increasing
amounts of time with the new system and ignore the old. That person
admitted that the problems associated with the new system were in-
triguing and represented personal growth, which he found quite reinforcing.

Atlantic management could not afford to have an established operation diminish at the expense of a new, unproven one, so two preventive
steps were taken. First, work assignments were redistributed so that time
would be available for critical steps. Second, feedback mechanisms were
set up to help monitor and regulate the rate at which projects progressed
through the two systems. Projections indicated that, eventually, all the
time of the individual critical to the system in Figure 5.2 would be needed
in the new subsystem, so a new employee was sought who could be trained
to do Steps 7, 9, and 10. An additional benefit of behavioral analysis was

derived when it was realized that the discriminative stimuli that signaled the onset of the next behavior in the process were not clearly displayed or as apparent for employees as they were for the system analyst. A simple color-coded procedure attached to the feedback mechanisms easily remedied that problem.

Many situations are more complex than that in the foregoing example. Nonetheless, the same principles apply, and the possibility of interaction increases with complexity. Therefore, the need for behavioral subsystem consideration is probably as great with multifaceted organizations as with smaller operations.

SUMMARY

From the foregoing examples it seems apparent that the behaviors of organisms are an essential part of social system function and, as such, rightly belong as part of any thorough description of a social system. If applied system theory is to provide the means for a comprehensive and integrative view of social as well as biological organizations and institutions, as writers such as M. A. Thompson (1975) suggest, behavioral subsystems must be considered when evaluation or planning occurs. This is not to say that the behaviors of system components are the only phenomenon of importance, but certainly they are part of the unified whole, which should not be overlooked.

Behavior management specialists who will be establishing new behavioral systems would do well to consider the behavioral subsystems within the internal networks of the systems that they are to create. Furthermore, the new systems will become part of external networks of systems, whose behavioral systems could be influenced by the outputs of the new systems. The techniques are available for behavior management specialists to take an ecological approach to behavioral control and to be aware during the planning process of the impact resulting from changes in the existing structure. Failure to do so could lead to limited benefits at one level and increased problems for related systems.

CHAPTER FIVE:
GUIDELINES FOR PRACTICAL APPLICATION

Guideline 5.1: When using the flowchart method for analyzing behavioral subsystems, do not be surprised if many decisions appear to be a choice of one of three or four possibilities rather than a yes/no situation. Actually, a decision with any number of alternatives can be broken down into a sequence of yes/no choices, but many people find that particular way of describing decisions cumbersome. If the number of alternatives to a decision is four or fewer, you may want to devise your own symbol for a decision point and have all the possible branches leading off from it.

Keep in mind that this business of identifying actions and analyzing decisions is very difficult for some people. (I have had students who have found it very difficult to even *follow a flowchart*). If you happen to be someone for whom flowcharting is an intolerable activity, you might seek out the help of a colleague who finds it "fun." I have found that highly organized, mathematically inclined, logical types generally enjoy flow-charting.

Guideline 5.2: When analyzing a behavioral subsystem using the flowchart method, keep in mind that the decisions made by people in the system are based upon some implicit or explicit criteria. Identification and standard-ization of those criteria are often neglected by system management; therefore, this is commonly an area where training is appropriate. The problem is not one of behavior management because employees can perform the correct responses, but rather, one of training because they just don't know how to correctly decide what they should do.

Often the decisions that have to be made in a process require that accurate, up-to-date information be available. As computer facilities be-come increasingly more common, you may find yourself recommending such equipment as an aid to behavior management.

Guideline 5.3: Flowcharting is almost always an iterative process with insertions and deletions occurring frequently until you arrive at a sequence that corresponds to what actually happens consistently within a system.

—To check on the accuracy of a flowchart, try using it to do the sequence of behaviors or to guide someone through them. If you can make appropriate decisions and accurately predict actions before they occur, your flowchart is probably adequate.

—Remember: Your flowchart is not sacred; therefore, it can be improved upon. However, managers are sometimes embarrassed to admit that the way they have been doing something is not the best or most efficient, so do not make them admit it. Just help them to discover possible improvements and be flexible.

Guideline 5.4: If analysis of a behavioral subsystem reveals several dif-ferent behaviors that should be changed, you may wish to initiate the changes one at a time. If, in fact, you are dealing with a system, the simple *change you make will result in unanticipated alterations in system functioning that you may need to deal with before going on to other planned changes in behavior.*

Also remember that the interconnectedness of behaviors in a system is likely to achieve unanticipated behavior changes in desired directions as well as in undesired directions. Capitalize on these changes by examining flowcharts for behaviors and decisions that are related either by discriminative stimuli or reinforcers.

Guideline 5.5: *When evaluating a system, you will want to examine the behavioral subsystems from the standpoint of effectiveness and efficiency. Anticipate having to recommend that:*

- *Discriminative stimuli that signal the appropriate occurrence of a behavior be made more reliable, distinctive, and /or apparent*
- *Reinforcement occur on a planned schedule rather than haphazardly*
- *Standardized flows or behavior sequences be agreed upon wherever possible and reasonable*
- *Flowcharts or simplified diagrams of behavior sequences be made available to employees*
- *Behaviors critical to system outcomes be specified as succinctly and clearly as possible*
- *Behavior sequences that cut across bureaucratic or administrative lines be made the responsibility of one person, for purposes of monitoring and reinforcing behaviors*

SIX
FEEDBACK: ENVIRONMENTAL, OUTPUT, AND PROCESS

In the behavioral system model (Figures 2.1 and 2.2) in Chapter Two, two feedback paths are apparent, one that arises from the output boundary of the system and another that comes from the receiving system. Actually, there is a third, called *process feedback*, which the behavior management specialist must recognize, and which operates within the system. These three feedback sources not only arise from different locations but, in each case, the type of feedback and its characteristics are essentially different. This chapter is devoted to a discussion of these differences, the various conceptualizations of feedback, and an explanation of feedback as it is used in the behavioral system framework. Before we consider the rationale for the three types of feedback, let us elaborate on them briefly.

PREVIEW GLOSSARY

Process Feedback: information flowing to system managers about the process being carried out within the system. Such information may include the rate at which certain tasks are done, how well they are done, the method used, and so forth. Examples: the director of a respiratory diseases treatment center will receive process feedback indicating how often inhalation therapy was given, by whom, and what the effects were; process feedback to the manager of a financial advisory group will include the stage or progress of each case, who is currently doing what on the case, what method is being used to calculate investment returns, and so forth.

Output Feedback: information flowing to system managers about the outputs leaving the system. Examples: the director of an employment training program will receive output feedback regarding how many students leave the program per week and what their specific skills are; the captain of a police department will receive weekly reports on how many citations were issued, how many arrests were made, and how many times assistance was given to citizens.

Environmental Feedback: information to system managers about the effects of system outputs on receiving systems. If goals exist, this information will relate to the specific conditions expressed in the goals. Examples: the dean of a business school will receive information from companies about how well graduates of the school are performing specific tasks in the companies; the fire chief will receive information from a house-to-house survey, indicating the impact that a radio and newspaper campaign has had on home fire safety measures; a garbage collection company will get feedback from customers about the neatness and promptness of pickup.

TYPES OF FEEDBACK

Process feedback arises from within the system and, as its name implies, provides information to the manager of the system about the process being carried out. *Output* feedback arises from the output boundary of the system and provides information to the manager of the system about the nature and rate of outputs. *Environmental* feedback comes from the receiving system(s) and provides information about the state of the receiving system or, viewed another way, about the consequences of the outputs upon the receiving system. None of these feedback mechanisms are necessarily present in a behavioral system but all are necessary for adequate control.

Perhaps because not all types of feedback are always present, not all systems theorists have agreed upon the definitions of feedback. Consider, for example, the following quotes:

For proper control, the feedback must always be negative ... When the feedback opposes the direction of the initial change that produced the feedback, the system tends to be stable. In contrast, when the returning feedback of energy supports the direction of initial change, the system tends to add to the initial energy gain and to be unstable (Parsegian, 1972).

The consequences of behavior may "feedback" into the organism. When they do so, they may change the probability that the behavior which produced them will occur again (Skinner, 1953).

Probably no other concept within systems theory has received as much attention yet presents such a confusing, contradictory posture as feedback. Is feedback negative? Or can it be positive in nature? What is the essential difference between positive and negative feedback: the nature of the signal or its effect? Does feedback control outputs, inputs, or system functioning? These are just a few of the questions one encounters when exploring the idea of feedback. As is obvious from the quotes above, the literature on feedback is inconsistent. If one wishes to employ the notion of feedback as a behavior management specialist, a logical, non-contradictory definition is necessary. The use of feedback in the behavioral system model hinges on the function of the system; hence, it begins with the relationship between goals and output feedback.

OUTPUT FEEDBACK

Goals and Output Feedback

Every system that possesses a clearly defined goal has the necessary ingredients for achieving system control through feedback. First, the goal (by definition) must specify a state (let us call it $State_2$) that the receiving system will attain. The state that it is in can currently be labeled $State_1$, and we would expect that goal direction would mean movement from $State_1$ to $State_2$. Second, the type and rate of outputs necessary from the system to move the receiving system from $State_1$ to $State_2$ can be identified by inference. Those necessary outputs are called the *desired output level* and can be visualized as a set of values having a high and low range as well as a time function. Figure 6.1 diagrammatically portrays this situation. The system's output level is at Point A initially, with Point B as its goal. At time T_1 its outputs must indicate that it is between the values of X and Y in order to be considered goal oriented. Outputs can be viewed as forces moving the system down the optimal path. A feedback or guidance subsystem that monitors outputs and assesses the system's state in relation to the desired output level is essential to keep the system within the optimal range and, hence, goal oriented. The feedback arising from such a subsystem will always be negative because of the operation of the mechanism. Actual level of performance is always subtracted from desired

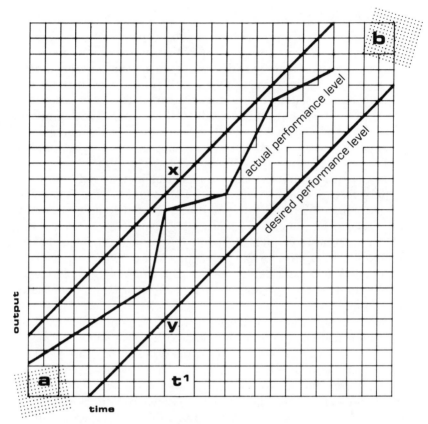

FIGURE 6.1   Diagrammatic representation of a negative feedback arrangement.

level of performance; hence, the use of the negative sign (−) and the term *negative feedback* (Forrester, 1968). Signals arising from such a mechanism are either zero (no difference between actual and desired performance) or some correction amount. That is, it will indicate by an error signal that the outputs are *not* within the range designated by the desired output level. This type of negative feedback can be viewed as *internal* because it arises from a sensor that is located within the system on the output boundary (Berrien, 1968), but we will call it *output feedback* so as not to confuse it with process feedback, which is also internal. It can be seen that such a concept of negative feedback is quite consistent with the earlier presented quotes of Laszlo et al. (1974), Parsegian (1972), and to a lesser extent with the statements of Skinner (1953).

An Example of Output Feedback

A concrete instance of output feedback occurred with a consultant firm, Environmental Assessments, Inc., that provided data for environmental impact statements. In order to meet financially imposed deadlines, one of the consultant firm's clients, Ski Enterprises, had to have a complete impact statement within 14 months. The goal, then, for Environmental Assessments, Inc., was: "By October 15, 1982, Ski Enterprises will have and be knowledgeable about a complete environmental impact statement, which includes... (nine specific items to be assessed were listed)."

Rather than submit the entire impact statement to Ski Enterprises at one time, Environmental Assessments, Inc., opted to present and explain each of the nine parts separately. They set up a schedule to present Item One between December 1 and January 15, Item Two between February 1 and March 30, and so on. This schedule represented the optimal path and the desired output level for Environmental Assessments, Inc. to follow. By establishing a goal and identifying an output rate that should meet that goal, Environmental Assessments, Inc., had set up an output feedback mechanism.

When the manager of Environmental Assessments, Inc., received the information that Item One of the impact statement would not be ready within the prescribed dates, he altered the system process to speed up the data collection. However, Items Two and Three would have been ready ahead of schedule, so the manager pulled researchers off the Ski Associates project and put them to work elsewhere until they were again needed for Item Four. With the aid of this feedback mechanism, the manager of Environmental Assessments, Inc., was able to monitor and control the system outputs such that the goal relating to Ski Enterprises could be met. Considering that Environment Assessments, Inc. was working on several other goals concurrently, feedback mechanisms were critical for proper management.

A behavior management specialist helped Environmental Assessments, Inc. set up the output feedback mechanism. He was initially asked to help them solve the problem of missed deadlines and confusion over project responsibilities. Upon discovering that no coordinated program existed within Environmental Associates, Inc., and that goals were not established, the behavior management specialist suggested a procedure of specific individual assignments and bonuses, contingent upon timely project completion. Without the goal and output feedback mechanism, behavior management techniques would have been only moderately effective.

It is obvious that output feedback of a negative nature is impossible unless goals are stated so that a desired output level can be derived. Feedback (negative) is impossible without a desired output level.

Output Feedback and Environmental Feedback

The output ensemble of a social system should be those products that, by inference or by evidence, are most likely to achieve the goals of the system. Hence, the desired output level is based upon a set of outputs that may permit goal attainment but that might not, given various changes in the situation. A situation can occur in which outputs are evaluated by the output feedback mechanism and found to be within the desired output level ranges, and as a result, no error signals (negative feedback) would arise; yet, the receiving system to which the outputs are directed is not utilizing them and the goal is not being reached. It is assumed here that the goals of the system in question are based upon an analysis of receiving system needs; therefore, the goal is to meet the identified needs of the receiving system. Consider, for example, Environmental Assessments, Inc., and their work for Ski Enterprises. It was assumed that the nine specific items would comprise a complete environmental impact statement. Suppose that this situation required two additional items that were not a part of the original nine. Environmental Assessments, Inc. would produce the nine items and would always receive output feedback indicating that the desired performance level was being met. It would need further feedback from Ski Enterprises to realize that nine items would not suffice for a complete impact statement in this particular case.

In order for Environmental Assessments, Inc. to become functional, it must adapt, which is to say that it must select new outputs that are more accurately related to the needs of the receiving system than were those previously produced. It is necessary for the system to have information from the receiving system that its outputs are or are not adequate and that needs are or are not being met. This leads to the notion that a second type and source of feedback is necessary, in addition to output feedback. This second type, which arises from a sensor in the receiving system, can be called *environmental* feedback because it returns across the interface with the receiving system and enters the system. Before going on to environmental feedback, we should briefly examine two new terms.

PREVIEW GLOSSARY

Mediated Feedback Loop: a process, output, or environmental feedback mechanism that has a human component for receiving the information and deciding the extent of the change (if any) in system process or output; in nonmediated loops the change occurs automatically. Examples : the director of a hospital laboratory got daily feedback on the rate at which reports left the lab; on one occasion he immediately changed a procedure when 12-hour delays occurred, yet on another occasion he waited 2 additional days to see if 12-hour delays would continue.

Feedback Sensor: *the device used to secure and feed information back to system management. Examples: an electronic counter senses the number of cars leaving a national park (output) and feeds the information to a computer that permits a set number of entrance passes to be sold; a counselor (sensor) visits the job sites (receiving system) of adult retardates from a "community living program" and gathers performance data, which the program director uses to guide further training; a color-coded case progress board (sensor) is updated at 12:00 and 5:00 P.M. by employees working on various aspects of contracts in a tax consultant firm.*

ENVIRONMENTAL FEEDBACK

Environmental feedback in social systems is often positive in nature. Note that we said it is "positive in nature," not that the feedback mechanism employs an additive process resulting in the use of a plus (+) sign and a constant increase. By saying that it is "positive in nature," we mean that the information feedback indicates a shift in the desired direction, is encouraging, or is highly valued. For example, Ski Enterprises may report to Environmental Assessments, Inc. that the impact statement was " . . . excellent . . . perfectly suited for their needs." Feedback such as this can be considered to be positive in nature.

The *runaway* concept of Laszlo et al. (1974) is not applicable when such positive feedback occurs. A positive feedback signal has runaway potential only *when it automatically increases the output of the system.* Most social systems have mediated feedback loops, however, which require that the feedback attain a certain level or frequency before a change in output occurs.

It seems clear, then, that output feedback mechanisms monitor the output of a system by utilizing a desired output level that permits only negative feedback, that is, an error signal, whereas the environmental feedback mechanism monitors the effect of one system's output on another system.

A careful reading of the quotes presented earlier in this chapter would give rise to the negative versus positive and output versus environmental feedback questions, but it would also leave open the question of whether feedback is the same as the psychological concept of *reinforcer* or a different entity altogether.

Feedback and Reinforcement

Confusion in terminology and definitions appearing in current literature can lead one to assert that: (1) feedback is a reinforcer, (2) reinforcers are feedback, and yet (3) feedback can be different from a reinforcer. Let us investigate each assertion individually to show how they can be true.

First, how can feedback be a reinforcer? Ferster et al. (1975) define a reinforcer as "the event which increases the frequency of the performance it immediately follows." Further elaboration is provided by Reynolds (1968):

> A second class of stimuli, the *reinforcing* stimuli, or *reinforcers*, is composed of environmental events which follow responses. Reinforcing stimuli increase the frequency of the responses they follow; they increase the probability that these responses will reoccur in the future behavior of the organism.

Does feedback follow a response? Yes, many examples of this sequence are available. In the case of a person steering a compass course on a ship, steering responses are followed by feedback at regular intervals. In a similar manner, lecturers receive comments about their verbal behavior after the lecture, not before. Do the rates of certain responses increase when followed by feedback? Yes; "on-target" steering responses increase for the person steering the ship when feedback occurs as a stimulus. If the probability of on-target responses increases when followed by feedback, by definition, feedback must be a reinforcer. Skinner (1953), in fact, refers to feedback as a conditioned reinforcer:

> In rifle practice, for example, extremely small scale properties of responses are differentially reinforced by a hit or a miss. Properties of this magnitude can be selected only if the differential reinforcement is immediate. But even when a hit can be seen by the rifleman, the report is delayed by the time which the bullet takes to reach the target. Possibly this gap is bridged by continual reinforcement from the "feel" of the shot. The rifleman eventually "knows" before the target is hit whether the shot was good or bad. His own behavior generates a stimulating feedback, certain forms of which are followed by hits, others by misses. . . . This does not mean that the rifleman will continue to shoot well . . . even though he receives no report of the effect upon the target or pins. The report is needed to maintain the conditioned reinforcing power of the feedback.

From the psychological standpoint, such a position seems consistent with explanations of feedback found in the systems' literature, which was discussed previously.

Feedback appears to fit the definition of reinforcement, but can it be turned about so that reinforcement is feedback? As we saw in his quote, Skinner (1953) has referred to reinforcement as a feedback process. In his interpretation of Hull's position, Hilgard (1956) stated, "Hull's position can be assimilated to an information theory. The minimum reinforcement necessary for habit strength is that required for information, for feedback; . . . "

We can deduce from this statement that consequences of behavior influencing probability of that behavior do so through the process of feedback. Therefore, if reinforcers are not, in fact, feedback, reinforcement at least includes a feedback process within its operation.

Now, let us explore some of the ways in which feedback can be different from reinforcers or reinforcement. The process of reinforcement is often represented symbolically by the following formula:

$$R \rightarrow S^R$$

The R is a response performed by the organism, and the S^R is the reinforcer that influences the probability of the R. When psychologists speak of the "consequences of behavior," they are referring to the S^R, the change in the environment arising as a consequence of the R. If we look back at Skinner's (1953) statement, "The consequences of behavior may 'feed back' into the organism," we can conclude that the information transmitted to the control center of the organism concerns the *consequences* of the behavior, or the S^R. A reinforcer simply provides information about the consequences or effects of the response on the environment. It is important to note that the information fed back to the organism in the form of a reinforcer reduces the uncertainty about the S^R but not about the R.

However, the many examples of feedback illustrate it as information dealing solely with the R, not the S^R. Take, for instance, Berrien's (1968) discussion of feedback. Although he does not specifically define feedback, he uses an example in which a sensor monitors the output of the system. This is very different from a sensor that monitors the consequences of a certain behavior. It is reasonable to assume that, before one could receive and use information about the S^R, it would be necessary to have information, that is, no uncertainty, about the R. Feedback mechanisms can provide information to the system about type, quantity, and quality of the output (R) or the consequences (S^R) of the behavior performed. It is in this manner that the author is regarding feedback and reinforcement as being different, and it is also for this reason that he suggests a behavioral system model utilizing dual feedback subsystems: one internal that monitors output and gives rise to a negative signal, and the other external that monitors the effect of the system on its environment and that can be positive or negative.

Therefore, output feedback, which is predominantly negative in order to be functional, should not be considered as reinforcement. It does not provide information to the system about the consequences of the system's behavior on the environment. However, environmental feedback that is related to the goals of a system can be either positive or negative in nature and, according to earlier definitions of *goal*, must relate to changes in the environment of other systems. Hence, environmental feedback can be synonymous within the construct, *reinforcement*.

The Thermostat as a Confusing Example

The thermostat on a furnace has been the classical, technological example of a common feedback mechanism. A critical examination of this concrete instance of feedback, in light of the foregoing discussion, will reveal some possible misconceptions. First, unlike most social systems, the mechanism is automated. The electrical signal produced by the sensor in the thermostat controls the furnace, but what is it monitoring and what does it control? That seems to depend upon the author and the type of thermostat. Mayr (1970) specifically referred to the thermostat as monitoring output and controlling input to control output, yet this seems confusing. The typical wall thermostat is *intentionally* placed at a distance from the furnace outlet so that it *cannot measure* output, but rather the effect of that output on the environment, which is to say that a thermostat appears to be an environmental feedback sensor located within the receiving system. The information that it provides is about the state of the environment, that is, "the receiving system needs more/less heat." However, Mayr (1970) was not referring to the typical zone control thermostat that is used in most modern homes; he was referring to a thermostat on the furnace that does measure and control output. When discussing feedback, many authors will either lump all feedback together or ignore one type or the other.

As the thermostat-furnace example illustrates, systems do not always have both environmental and output feedback mechanisms, nor are those that have such mechanisms identical in operation. Feedback is a means for controlling a system, and different systems have varying degrees of control, especially within the social domain. The behavior manager who provides for goals and environmental feedback as well as for output specifications and output feedback has established control mechanisms that will enhance system functioning, consonant with original designs. However, the third feedback type, *process*, should be considered.

PROCESS FEEDBACK

The third feedback mechanism necessary for proper functioning of behavioral systems operates within the system and is used to monitor the processes taking place. You will recall that the process of a system is the sequence of events between input and output. In order to produce certain outputs, it is assumed that specific processes must take place. The executive (decider) function of the system must have input about what processes are actually occurring in order to control the outputs and, hence, achieve the goals of the system. Since processes in behavioral systems are often sequences of behaviors, process feedback is often information about what behaviors are occurring within the system.

An instance of process feedback occurred in the Environmental Assessments, Inc. situation. You will recall that nine items of information had to be outputted. In order to output each item, a certain set of steps was identified and listed on a chart that was known around the office as an "operations board." This chart was actually a process feedback mechanism for the manager of Environmental Assessments, Inc. It provided information about what steps had been completed, which steps were currently being done, and which researchers were working on which steps. The possession of that information allowed the manager to control the process and hence, the outputs and further, the achievement of the goal.

VARIABLES TO BE CONSIDERED IN FEEDBACK

The simple existence of a feedback mechanism is not a sufficient condition to guarantee control over system functioning. At least two variables, *information specificity* and *frequency*, will influence the extent to which a system can be controlled through feedback.

Information specificity refers to the degree of correspondence between what is fed back and what actually happens. In output feedback, for example, nonspecific feedback may simply report an increase when, in fact, the output rate may have doubled. A specific feedback mechanism would report the amount of the increase quantitatively. With specific information, feedback decisions can be made that can "fine tune" the system, whereas, with nonspecific information feedback, only gross adjustments can be accomplished.

Like specificity of information, the frequency of the feedback interval plays a major role in the degree to which a system can be controlled. Keep in mind that corrections to the system can occur with accuracy only when feedback is received. Therefore, the more often feedback occurs, the more corrections to the system can be made. Let us look at a concrete instance of this. If the manager of Environmental Assessments, Inc. received process feedback on a three-week interval, the system would have considerable chance to go astray before corrections could be made. At the same time, suppose an engineer at Environmental Assessments, Inc. began taking water percolation measures from four sites instead of a standardly prescribed eight sites. If a process feedback mechanism provided information to the manager on a four-day instead of a three-week interval, this mistake could be caught before critical time and money were lost and before the output was seriously affected.

VARIATIONS ON A THEME

In an earlier chapter we discussed the likelihood that systems would not have goals and, therefore, be managed on the basis of values. Behavior management specialists working with behavioral systems should anticipate such situations. It will be quite common to find feedback mechanisms operating even in the absence of goals. In fact, desired performance levels derived from values can be used to evaluate the appropriateness of actual performance levels. The problem, of course, in such a condition is that process, output, and environmental feedback are not coordinated to achieve a specific outcome. A manager could receive environmental feedback from the receiving system that had nothing to do with the products outputted to that receiving system or, worse yet, a manager could receive feedback that was always arranged to be pleasing or to rank high on that person's value hierarchy.

In an earlier chapter we used an example of a manager who sent out a questionnaire as an environmental feedback device. That manager valued highly the subjective praise and expressions of "good feelings" that were contained in the returned questionnaires and made certain that the process within the system resulted in workshop participants who were pleased with the experience. It is interesting to note that this particular manager had an output feedback mechanism that monitored the attendance of participants at workshop activities and also had process feedback that was delivered by an assistant once each afternoon and that was highly nonspecific. ("The people seem pretty happy with the workshop. No one slept during Mr. Atkinson's talk.") In addition, the manager had output feedback that was delivered by the workshop director and was specific about attendance only. Finally, there was environmental feedback that was secured through a questionnaire and that was focused on the emotional state of the participants. If any of the information fed back was not high on the manager's value hierarchy, revisions to the system would be made, which should result in more favorable information feedback. For example, the manager placed great value on attendance records that showed 95 percent or more of the participants at each activity. He revised the system so that certificates of attendance were placed in each participant's personnel file at the end of each workshop. This procedure seemed to be sufficient to result in the outputting of participants from the workshop who had attended 95 percent or more of the sessions.

UNSOLICITED ENVIRONMENTAL FEEDBACK

A particularly unfortunate situation in terms of system control occurs when managers of systems receive feedback through sensors that they did not devise and they they do not control. Keep in mind that, if the system in question had goals, unsolicited feedback *could* be ignored in favor of goal-related feedback from sensors placed by the system manager. If no goals exist, values will dictate how the system is managed. If information is fed back to the system at the discretion of someone *outside the system*, the degree to which the system responds to that feedback is the degree to which the system is controlled by an outside agent. The outside agent can ensure system control by providing highly valued feedback.

An example may help to clarify the situation we have just described. Imagine an industrial research lab that does not have goals. It receives requests from various engineering and development departments within the company and sends out reports after varying degrees of research have been completed. Often the reports sent out are simply reprints of previous studies. These are sometimes marginally relevant to the request and are not up-to-date. For some reason, a computer reference search was completed for a report requested by one of the engineering departments. If the research lab had goals, a sensor could be placed in the engineering department, and it could be determined if the output of a report with a computer reference search helped to achieve the goal. The research lab did not have goals, nor did it solicit environmental feedback, so the engineering department head decided to provide some unsolicited feedback. First, he took the head of the research lab to lunch, "in appreciation for the excellent report you did for us." Second, he made a point of mentioning that the division vice-president had heard about the excellent report and was pleased with the display of interdepartmental cooperation. The research lab manager now had unsolicited environmental feedback to the effect that, as a consequence of producing a report with a computer reference search, the engineering department head was of a mind to take him to lunch and, further, the vice-president was in a pleased state of mind over the interdepartmental cooperation. Both of these pieces of feedback are quite likely to be high on the research lab manager's hierarchy and to have an influence on subsequent operation of the research lab, especially when it comes to that particular engineering department.

FEEDBACK AND THE
BEHAVIOR MANAGEMENT SPECIALIST

At this point, we have a fairly good grasp of how feedback fits into the framework for behavioral systems. However, one further example may be useful to illustrate the three types of feedback and how feedback, as a part of the behavioral system framework, can be useful to the behavior management specialist.

Once again, let's draw upon the experiences of Lawrence Adams in his role as a behavior management consultant. Adams was retained by an airline company to establish the use of behavioral techniques in a flight training program. The company's initial interest was in the use of behavioral analysis and organizational behavior management.

A very superficial system analysis revealed to Adams that the flight training program received inputs in the form of company pilots, navigators, and engineers. They went through two major in-line subsystems within the flight training program that were differentiated primarily on the basis of instructional content and technique. The first subsystem amounted to 60 hours of lectures on specific aircraft technology and engineering. The second subsystem encompassed 60 hours of practice and problem-solving seminars with nonfunctioning mockups. After completing the 120-hour program, students were outputted to a simulator training program, which was essentially another system. Although the director of the flight training program could express some general purposes for his system, there were no goals nor was there an environmental feedback mechanism connecting the flight training program and the simulator training program. Furthermore, the director of the flight training program did not "interfere" with his instructors; hence, there was no process feedback, and output feedback was limited to exam scores derived from tests that had neither been standardized nor validated.

It was into this situation that the director of the flight training program wanted Adams to insert a behavior modification program to "motivate the students" and "improve the image of the program." Adams felt he could establish a token economy of sorts as long as reinforcers could be identified and provided that instructors would cooperate in maintaining the contingencies. He also believed, however, that the system, if not changed, would eventually interfere with any behavior management program.

Adams made a presentation to the director and three assistant directors, in which he outlined the nature and function of goals, environmental feedback, output feedback, and process feedback. In addition, he stressed the necessity of viewing the simulator training program as the receiving system for the flight training program.

It came as no surprise to Adams that the director of the flight training program did not want to work with the group from the simulator training program. They were rival divisions within the company when it came to recognition and budgets. Realizing the limitations imposed by such parochial politics, Adams, nevertheless, established several goals that were focused on the performance of students in the simulators. With the help of the instructors in the flight training program, he identified the criteria that each student would have to meet before being outputted to the simulator training program. A standardized testing program was set up so that feedback was always available about the students to be outputted. Next, a variety of taped and live lectures, films, film strips, individualized instructional units, and problem-solving tasks were developed, with performance measures tailored to each one. Lawrence convinced the director that monitoring which tasks were being done by whom, in how much time, and with what results was not interference with his instructors but rather, information necessary for evaluation and control over the program. A chart that was updated daily at 12:00 noon and 4:30 P.M. detailed this information. The system was now operating with process and output feedback mechanisms.

After establishing a token economy that was demonstrated to improve students' performance over baseline levels, Adams designed a data sheet that he asked the assistant director of the simulator training program to complete and return once a week. The data sheet provided information about several performance measures taken in the simulators and the time devoted to each skill area. As crude and limited as it might be, an environmental feedback mechanism was now operating between the flight training program and its receiving system, the simulator training program.

Adams could now set up behavior management programs that would support and be supported by the established goals of the flight training program. The effects of behavior change programs could be evaluated in terms of process, output, and environmental feedback as well as individual behavior rate data. In short, Adams used the behavioral system framework and especially the concepts of feedback to attain an ecological perspective from which to initiate and evaluate behavior management attempts.

CHAPTER SIX: GUIDELINES
FOR PRACTICAL APPLICATION

Guideline 6.1: Keep in mind that behavior change itself requires a feedback loop, that is, the manager of the behavior change must have information about the rate and direction of behaviors to be changed. Be careful not to confuse this with process or output feedback of the system in which the behavior occurs.

— Remember that the behavior change you are carrying out in a system should benefit the system; therefore, the system process or outputs should improve in some manner. Without process or output feedback, you (and the system managers) will not know what effect the behavior change has had on system functioning.

— Expect that most existing systems that turn out intangible outputs (therapy, counseling, child care, training, and so forth) will not have output or environmental feedback loops.

— If the system in which you are going to change behavior does not have an output feedback loop, you may have to establish one, even though the connection to your behavior change program is not direct (see the discussion of first and second order measures in Chapter Ten).

— Expect that, if they have feedback at all, most systems that you encounter will have "problem only" feedback. In such cases the management will not want information about how well things are going but will only want feedback about problems that have arisen. The danger with this arrangement is that, by the time problems become visible, the extent of damage or cost may have exceeded that of a feedback mechanism that would have forestalled the problem.

Guideline 6.2: Remember that "information costs," so, as a result, feedback loops place a financial burden on the system in excess of that necessary to carry out process. Furthermore, the costs of getting the appropriate information to feed back about process, outputs, or environmental effects are often hidden costs that are not easily related to productivity. If behavior change is to be cost-effective, you must develop feedback loops that provide the specific information needed at the lowest cost possible to permit control of the behavior change and the system.

There are critical questions to be answered as you set up a feedback mechanism:

• Is it to be process, output, or environmental feedback?

- *What is the minimal information to be fed back in order to evaluate and control the system?*
- *What is the longest possible feedback interval without losing control over the system?*
- *How can the information to be fed back be efficiently and accurately secured?*
- *What is the most effective procedure for feeding the information back to managers?*
- *How does (Can . . .) the managers use the information that is fed back?*

Guideline 6.3: *Keep in mind that feedback implies evaluation, which in turn, implies judgment to most people. Negative judgment generally means criticism, loss of power, money, and so forth. You should expect that the establishment of feedback loops will be met by system members with caution and, perhaps, avoidance.*

— *Assurances from you to system members that feedback is only used to evaluate and control system functioning will probably fall on deaf ears.*

— *Remember: Action speaks louder than words. Make certain that initial use of the feedback mechanism results in positive reinforcement for system members if system functioning improves.*

— *Anticipate a period of turmoil and readjustment among system members if no feedback was previously available. Reinforce adjustment attempts that are indicated by feedback and that may improve system functioning.*

Guideline 6.4: *When evaluating a system, look for feedback loops that were not set up (and are not controlled) by the managers of the system.*

— *Conflicting judgments regarding system functioning are often the result of false, irrelevant, or nonspecific feedback.*

— *Remember: In a system without goals, the values of managers will dictate system responses to feedback. Eventually, the only feedback loops operating will be those that relate to management values.*

Guideline 6.5: *When designing or planning a system, it is easy to short-change feedback mechanisms after having spent considerable time on goals and process. You can be certain that, once a new system is initiated, managers will not have the time or the perspective to develop feedback mechanisms. For the sake of system control, include complete plans for feedback in any system proposal (see Chapter Eight).*

The coordination of process, output, and environmental feedback is critical to proper system functioning. Whether analyzing, evaluating or planning a system, look to see that these three feedback mechanisms are arranged to support each other and to help the system maintain goal or target orientation.

SEVEN
BEHAVIORAL SYSTEM
NEEDS ASSESSMENT

As the conceptual framework associated with the behavioral system model in Figure 2.1 has been developed and discussed in the previous chapters, it should have become apparent that system goals and functions depend upon the needs of receiving systems. In order for a system to have meaningful goals, an assessment of receiving system needs has to have been conducted.

The behavior management specialist who must identify or design changes in behavioral systems is constantly confronted with the problems associated with the initial assessment of system needs, and subsequently, the design of programs that meet those needs. In this age of raised public consciousness and community involvement, it is risky business, indeed, to design and implement programs with only an ambiguous definition of the needs to be met by the program. In both the public and private sector, misuse of resources on ineffective programs is to be rigorously avoided, yet program planners and managers are often unable to identify precisely the needs to be met by a specific program simply because a conceptually sound methodology for determining those needs is not readily available. How does one identify the needs of a community, a law enforcement agency, an agricultural cooperative, a public or private corporation, or any of the other organizations that can be called behavioral systems?

It is important to note at this point that the emphasis in this chapter is on needs assessment of behavioral systems, not of sets of individuals that

Parts of this chapter were taken from R. L. Morasky & D. Amick, "Social Systems Needs Assessment," in *Long Range Planning*, 1978, *11*. Copyright 1978 by Pergamon Press, Ltd. Reprinted by permission of Pergamon Press, Ltd.

can be grouped on the basis of common characteristics. For example, a law enforcement agency has a function; its members interact and produce system outputs related to the function of the system. The population of people over age 65 is a set or group rather than a system unless interaction occurs between members to produce outputs, in which case a system would exist (that simply had elderly members). It is the purpose of this chapter to present a general strategy for assessing the needs of behavioral systems. Conceptually, the strategy is based on the logic and principles previously presented; therefore, before discussing the strategy itself, the stage must be set by identifying a few critical relationships and reviewing a few basic systems concepts.

WHAT ARE NEEDS?

Needs statements in program proposals often seem ill defined, poorly constructed, and confusing. These deficiencies may be due in part to the absence or lack of application of a conceptual framework, such as behavioral systems offer. To the system theorist, needs are not the same as demand projections, problem descriptions, or goals, and an understanding of their differences is essential to an adequate comprehension of what needs are.

Demand projections should be viewed as conditional statements describing the anticipated activity that would occur in a particular system, given a specific set of conditions and assumptions. Estimates of the number of people using a public recreation facility and the type of activities in which they will engage during the next two years is an example of a demand projection. A number of methods for estimating demand are available, and most are dependent upon data depicting previous participation in existing systems. Model building, standards development, or statistical prediction are common means for establishing demand projections. Such strategies provide information about what past use was and what future use might be but not necessarily what will be needed in order to permit that future use to occur. Even if demand data were useful, behavior management specialists are often involved in situations where previous use data are neither applicable nor available.

Like demand information, *problem identification* is often inappropriately viewed as synonymous with needs assessment. The logic seems to be that, once one identifies the problem, the needs will be readily apparent. If system problems are defined as deficiencies or excesses within the system, identifying the problem is only half of the needs assessment task. Descriptive data detailing the problems existing within a system are hardly sufficient information to know what is needed to remediate or resolve the problems.

In a previous chapter, goals were discussed from a systems viewpoint, and it should suffice to say here that *goals* are functional when they specify the state a system will be in when the problems are remediated or resolved. Again, the needs of a system are not the predicted use patterns (demands), the existing deficiencies or excesses (problems) in the system, nor the desired system states (goals). Rather, the needs of a system are those inputs to a system that are required in order for the system to meet demands, alleviate problems, or achieve goals.

If we view a system as "a set of objects together with relationships between the objects and between attributes" (Hall & Fagan, 1968), and if behavioral systems are generally open, that is, if they interact with other systems by receiving inputs and producing outputs, we can diagrammatically represent a system network, as in Figure 7.1. As illustrated, System A receives inputs from a number of input source systems and produces outputs to a number of receiving systems. If System A has a problem, due to demands, deficiencies, excesses, or whatever, this state of affairs will affect its receiving systems via the outputs produced. Because of the quantity or quality of the inputs received, the receiving systems of System A cannot function as desired. We can label the current problem or condition of System A as $State_1$. The condition in which we desire System A to be (wherein the problems do not exist and appropriate outputs are produced) is labeled $State_2$. The needs of System A, then, are whatever is required to move it from $State_1$ to $State_2$.

AIMS AND MAJOR TASKS OF NEEDS ASSESSMENT

The task of the behavior management specialist is to create or modify the input source systems to System A so that appropriate inputs are available, problems are alleviated, and a desired state is attained. Therefore, the task or objective of the needs assessment strategy is twofold: (1) to identify specific problems in the system network according to type, extent, location, and nature, and (2) to identify inputs required in order to alleviate the problems identified in step 1.

A specific example should help to clarify this systems-oriented explanation of needs assessment. Suppose that a large organization has a research department that should output new product performance data to a marketing department and to a product design department. The research department can be designated System A, as in Figure 7.1, and the marketing and product design departments are two of the receiving

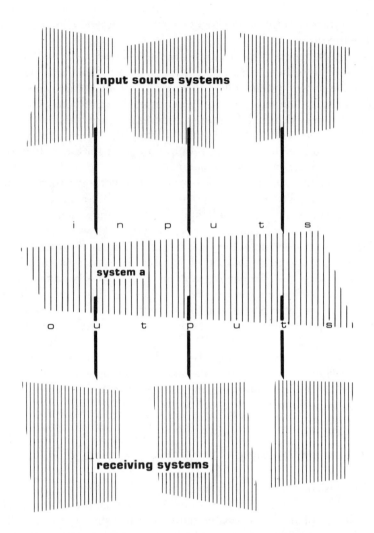

FIGURE 7.1 An open-system network.

systems. Assume that management believes a problem exists in the research department and that a consultant is engaged to prepare either a new network or a revision of the existing one. The consultant faces two questions: (1) what problems are there in the system network that relate to the process or outputs of the research department?, and (2) what must be provided to the research department in order to alleviate the problems in the network? The input to the research department may be a new organizational structure, new personnel, a revised budget, or any of a variety of other items that would produce the desired change. When the consultant has a reasonably accurate idea of the required inputs, the needs assessment phase of the planning has been successfully completed.

It is important to note, in this case, that the consultant must consider the relationship of the research department to other departments, not just its situation in isolation. Because superordinate and subordinate relationships are being dealt with, the consultant must be alert to several problems that can be inherent in certain needs assessment strategies not designed for application to systems.

PROBLEMS WITH NEEDS ASSESSMENT STRATEGIES

Several potential problems lie in the path of the behavior management specialist engaged in a needs assessment project. A primary obstacle can be limited perception of the system members who might be contacted for needs information. Specifically, it is probable that any given system will have gone through a process of goal displacement (Berelson & Steiner, 1964), which typically results in original goals being replaced by other orientations that were called targets in Chapter Three. These new targets often involve the accomplishment of certain processes or actions rather than the achievement of particular ends. If the members of the system offer opinions about deficiencies and needs in relation to internal operations but not in relation to the total network of system interactions, the needs being met will be appropriate to what is becoming an increasingly closed or nonfunctional system. However, it should certainly not be assumed that "felt needs" expressed by system members will be inappropriate in every case. The manager who is aware of the system network and the phenomenon of goal displacement should be in a position to judge the validity of needs that may be expressed.

On the other hand, even if system members are aware of the impact of one system upon another and the relationships illustrated in Figure 7.1, it is not likely that they will be fully aware of the various treatments, methods, and materials available for alleviating deficiencies. For instance, suppose that in Figure 7.1, System A has a problem that is preventing it from providing the proper outputs to its receiving systems. It, therefore, needs some special input from one or more of its input source systems. This special input could be in the form of materials, personnel, information, or almost anything else. If the behavior manager surveys the members of System A to determine what they think they need, the possibility exists that an effective input will be overlooked simply because the system members are not aware of it as a potential input. Again, as with the problem of goal displacement, system members may not be the best sources of specific needs information.

A third problem that is often overlooked in needs assessment strategies is that the individuals surveyed for needs information may not know the specific effects of inputs that are commonly believed to be needed. In most areas of the social and behavioral sciences, there have been some cause and effect relationships demonstrated that were sometimes unpredictable and often entirely surprising. In other cases, effects of certain actions have been shown to be counterintuitive, that is, what intuition dictates should occur does not, but, in fact, the effect is something that intuition says should not occur. It should not be anticipated that members of social systems will be cognizant of such outcomes; therefore, one would expect not to see unusual items identified in a needs assessment survey given only to system members. It may be advisable for the behavior manager to consult experts in a particular field for needs information once the desired effect or state is known.

The problems of needs assessment identified above suggest the necessity for a conceptual framework for a needs assessment strategy that permits the collection of data from a variety of relevant sources. It is certainly appropriate to expect to acquire certain information from specific members of behavioral systems, but it is not axiomatic that total needs assessment data should be attained only from system members. As illustrated in the strategy that follows, only those system members who play certain roles are prime sources of particular needs assessment data.

A NEEDS ASSESSMENT STRATEGY

The logic of the needs assessment strategy described here is based on the premise associated with systems theory that social systems are open and that their outputs flow to other systems and influence those systems. An assessment of the needs of any system is an identification of the inputs that a system needs in order to output the appropriate products to other systems and permit those systems to achieve desired states or conditions. In terms of the diagram in Figure 7.1, the needs of System A are dependent upon the conditions prevailing in the receiving systems.

Figure 7.2 is a flowchart of a generalized needs assessment strategy, based on systems theory concepts. The rectangles in Figure 7.2 represent actions to be taken, and the diamonds indicate decision points. It is assumed that the behavior manager has identified the system that allegedly has needs before attempting to use the flowchart. Each step in Figure 7.2 is numbered and the steps are described as follows:

FIGURE 7.2 Flowchart of needs assessment strategy.

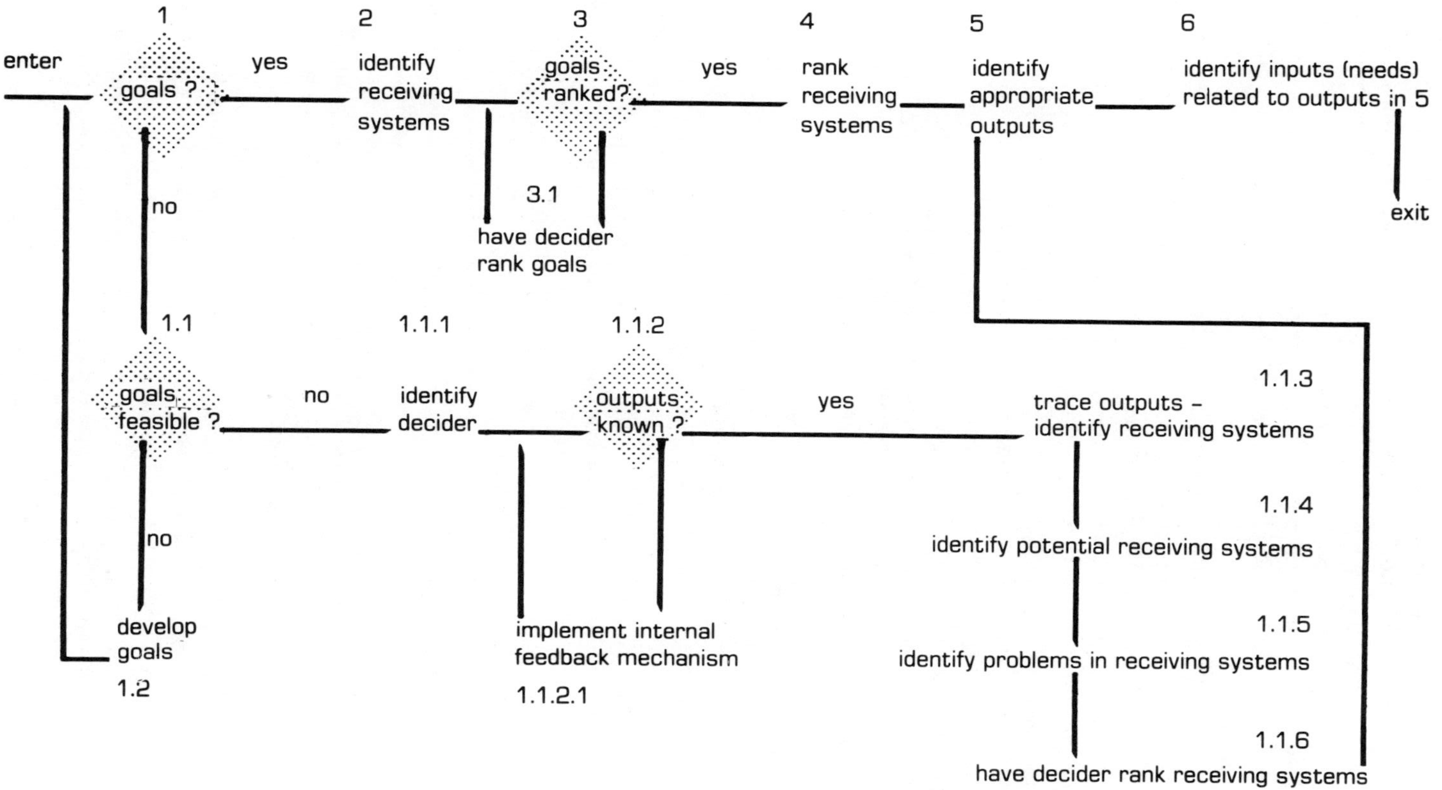

Step 1: The initial task for the behavior manager is to make a decision as to whether or not the system in question has goals. Goals have been rather rigidly defined in the systems sense, so some detailed probing of the system is essential in order to make an accurate decision. This choice point leads to two different paths that converge only after several intervening steps have been completed. We will discuss the affirmative choice and path first.

Step 2: Since the system has goals, the systems that receive its outputs can readily be identified. At this step, one simply identifies those systems in Figure 7.1 that are labeled the Receiving Systems.

Step 3: Another decision needs to be made at this point: are the goals of the system ranked according to their respective priorities?

Step 3.1: If the goals are not rank ordered, the behavior manager must ask the decider of the system to identify priorities and rank the goals. Recall that the decider of a system is the executive function that controls system processes, boundaries, inputs, outputs, and purposes and that the decider need not be a single person but can be a shared role accomplished by different persons or groups at different times. If the goals simply cannot be ranked, then the behavior manager must go on to Step 4, where a similar end must be achieved.

Step 4: If the goals are rank ordered, it should be possible for the behavior manager to identify the corresponding rank order of the receiving systems. That is the action taken in this step; the receiving systems identified in Step 2 are now placed in some order of preference. If the goals were not ranked in Step 3.1, the decider must again be consulted and requested to rank order the receiving systems. At this point, the priorities given will probably be based upon the value structure of the decider, which, in turn, can depend upon the environmental feedback flowing from the respective receiving systems to the system and, hence, to the decider.

Step 5: The behavior manager can now identify the appropriate outputs that the system in question must produce in order for the goals to be met. In addition, the outputs can be rank ordered according to the goal and receiving system priorities achieved in the previous step. Those outputs flowing to the highest-ranked receiving systems are most important and other outputs receive lower priorities, according to the ranks of the systems to which they flow.

Selection of the correct output to produce the desired effect will often necessitate consultation with experts in various fields. Individuals with various system affiliations may strongly suggest that certain outputs are obviously needed, and this may be accompanied by implicit assumptions about outcomes. The conscientious behavior manager would do well to keep the desired ends in mind and to seek out authoritative information as to which outputs have been shown to elicit the preferred changes in the receiving systems. In Figure 7.1, this corresponds to identifying the outputs flowing from System A to the receiving systems of System A.

At Step 5, the two separate paths begun at Step 1 converge, so our discussion will jump to Step. 1.1 and progress back to Step 5.

Step 1.1: If the decision at Step 1 was that goals do not exist, the behavior manager must decide at this step whether or not there is sufficient control over system contingencies to effect the establishment of goals.

Step 1.2: The development of goals follows the decision that such an administrative operation is feasible. Once goals have been developed, the behavior manager can return to Step 1 and proceed along the path appropriate to existing goals.

Step 1.1.1: Should the decision at Step 1.1 be that the establishment of goals is not feasible, the behavior manager must then identify the personnel of the system in question. Recall that this probably will be several people working at parallel levels or different individuals managing the system at different times.

Step 1.1.2: The decision to be made here is whether or not the outputs from the system in question are known.

Step 1.1.2.1: If an accurate accounting of outputs is not available, the behavior manager should establish and implement feedback mechanisms that will provide information to the decider about the type and rate of outputs produced. This necessitates the identification of the output boundary of the system and the establishment of an appropriate sensor that can monitor outputs leaving the system. This step will result in the identification of current outputs and permit the planner to go on to Step 1.1.3.

Step 1.1.3: The objective of this step is to identify the receiving systems to which the outputs of the system flow. This can be accomplished by tracing the output flow and identifying the first system that actually processes the output, as opposed to simply serving as an intervening system for the purpose of transmittal or transportation of the output between systems.

Step 1.1.4: At this point, *potential* receiving systems should be identified. It is assumed that the system in question could output to systems that are not currently linked to it.

Step 1.1.5: The task in this step is to determine the problems that exist in the identified receiving systems. The problems of concern are those related to the outputs flowing from the system in question. In terms of Figure 7.1, the problems to be identified are those existing in the receiving systems on the right side of the figure. Only the problems that have some relationship to the outputs from System A are of importance. Other problems might exist, but if System A could not influence them, they are not of concern in this particular needs assessment.

Step 1.1.6: The actions in this step are similar to those in Step 4, that is, the decider must rank order the actual and potential receiving systems. With this task complete, the flow progresses to Step 5, which was discussed previously.

Step 6: Once the appropriate outputs from the system in question have been identified in Step 5, the behavior manager must determine what *inputs* must flow *to* that system. One should not think of "inputs" as only material objects. Designs for structural reorganization, personnel changes, budget supplements, contingencies, and training all come under the heading of *inputs*. These are the needs of the system in question. Before settling on a specific set, the behavior manager must consider alternative inputs as well as the practicality of each, given the resources available. The input ensemble that is finally designated as "needed" will be, in most cases, a compromise between the ideal and the practical and not necessarily the obvious choice, given an absence of constraints. The following example should help the reader to generalize from an overview of a broad strategy to actual circumstances.

AN APPLICATION OF THE ASSESSMENT STRATEGY

In the United States, there is an extensive nonprofit organization called Big Brothers and Sisters, which coordinates the matching of volunteer adults with children who lack a particular adult model. The outcome of this association is believed to be a better adjusted young person than might have resulted with the absence of the adult influence. In 1976 a regional unit of the Big Brother/Big Sister Organization requested in-service training help for the Big Brothers and Sisters. The leaders of the organization believed that the Little Brothers and Sisters (hereafter referred to as "Littles") were presenting problems that the Big Brothers and Sisters (hereafter referred to as Bigs) were not trained to handle, in most cases. Therefore, the administration came to the conclusion that the Bigs needed training, but the exact nature and content of the training was unknown. It appeared to be an excellent situation in which to apply the needs assessment strategy described previously.

The first step was to conceptualize the system with which we were working and which allegedly had needs. It was possible to perceive the regional unit as a system, with the Big-Little pairings being its primary output along with other less prominent outputs such as publicity, organizational affiliation, group activities, and so forth. The identified problem, however, was not with the organization's ability to output pairings but rather with the difficulties encountered and presented by the Littles. On the basis of this general description of the problem, it was decided that the system in question should be each Big/Little pairing. We were then dealing with several two-person systems rather than one multiple-person system.

Having conceptualized the system in this way, it was possible to enter the flowchart in Figure 7.2 and to progress through the strategy. Step 1 resulted in a "no" response; most Big/Little systems do not have specific, manifest goals that can be readily communicated. This information was initially determined by questioning a sample of the population and later confirmed by surveying the entire set of systems.

The response to Step 1.1 was also a "no." No one seemed to have sufficient contingency control to make the mandatory setting of goals a feasible alternative.

Step 1.1.1 necessitated the identification of the system decider. Although the director of the regional unit performed the function of decider of the parent organization or suprasystem, the actual deciders of the two-person systems in question seemed to be the Bigs. An interesting problem arose at this point because it could be argued that the director was the decider of each system by virtue of the fact that he simply told the Big to spend time with the Little. The Big could carry out this process with no control over the resulting inputs or outputs and, therefore, not be the decider. An alternative argument was that both the Big and the Little shared the decider role with no control exerted by the director of the parent organization. A cursory analysis of several Big/Little systems revealed that the Big was quite probably the decider. More importantly, it was the opinion of the director that the systems should operate with the Big as decider even if they were not doing so at the present.

At Step 1.1.2 it was decided that, in a general sense, the outputs of the Big/Little systems were known. After discussion with several Big Brothers and the organization director, the desired outputs of the systems could be described as Little Brothers/Sisters with behavior repertoires or patterns that were socially acceptable. This general definition of output obviously encompassed a very large number of behaviors and said nothing about specific behaviors being developed in specific systems. Nonetheless, it was decided that Steps 1.1.3 and 1.1.4 could be completed quite adequately with this degree of output identification.

The following systems were identified in Steps 1.1.3 and 1.1.4 as being those that receive the behaviors of the Little: school, family, peers, legal authorities, employer, adults in general, self, and the Big Brother or Sister. Note that not all of these are systems; peers, for instance, are actually a "set" of individuals grouped according to arbitrarily selected characteristics. Each of these was divided into subsystems or subgroups, if appropriate; for example, family was divided into parent and sibling subsystems.

The objective in Step 1.1.5 was to determine in which receiving systems there were problems related to the behavior of the Little Brother or Sister. In order to achieve this data the entire population of Bigs in the regional unit was formally interviewed by a trained interviewer, utilizing a standardized format. Several questions in the interview dealt with current problems between the Little's behavior and a particular system. The percent of interviewees responding with either a "yes, there is a problem" or "I don't know" to questions about various systems is shown in Figure 7.3. Figure 7.4 shows similar data for questions about future (5 years hence) problems. For each affirmative response, the interviewee was asked to recite a specific instance exemplifying the type of problem perceived.

During the interviews, respondents were also asked to rank order the receiving systems with problems, according to their importance or criticality. Hence, by the completion of Step 1.1.6, we knew which systems were perceived by the Bigs as possibly needing new outputs from the Littles, and which systems were regarded as most important to consider initially. It is interesting to note that, should the "don't know" response rate have been considerably higher than the "yes" rate, we would still have had useful data. Since the Bigs were intended to be the deciders in the Big/Little systems, they should have had information about the identified receiving systems. The lack of such information, illustrated by "don't know" responses, would indicate the need for environmental or external feedback mechanisms from each receiving system to the Big. With proper feedback, the Big could identify the receiving systems that were experiencing difficulties with the outputs produced. As it turned out in this particular situation, "don't know" responses were minimal.

The data represented in Figure 7.3 indicate that four systems were perceived by the Bigs as being definite problem areas for the Littles. In order, these were the self, schoolwork, parent, and teacher. Furthermore, the system labeled "self" was identified in the interviews as being the highest priority system with which to deal. Hence, the receiving system most often identified as having problems was also most often identified as having the highest priority, a usual but not necessary condition. Step 5 required that the outputs from the Big/Little system to the "self" (Little), schoolwork, parent, and teacher be identified.

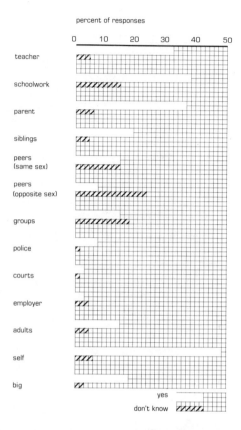

FIGURE 7.3   Percent of "yes" and "don't know" responses to questions concerning current problems in receiving systems.

The specific examples collected in the interviews suggested three major problem areas with "self": self-concept, self-esteem, and self-confidence. In a general sense, then, the outputs of the Big/Little system should have been a Little with behaviors that reflected an accurate self-concept, appropriate self-esteem, and appropriate self-confidence. For the sake of brevity, the specific target behaviors are not listed here but were critical to a concise description of the output ensemble. This procedure of identifying the outputs to flow from the Big/Little system to the receiving system was also completed for the teacher and schoolwork

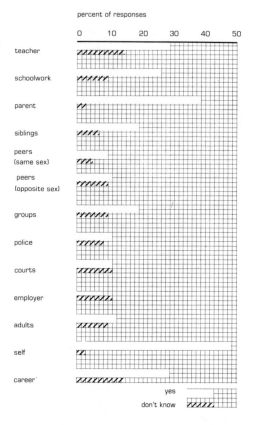

percent of responses

FIGURE 7.4 Percent of "yes" and "don't know" responses to questions concerning future problems in receiving systems.

systems. Interviews revealed that, although problems existed with the parent system, the Bigs did not feel that the Big/Little system could or should have an influence in that area.

It was assumed that the Big/Little systems, in their existing states, could not always output Littles with the desired behavioral repertoires identified in Step 5; therefore, those systems needed specific inputs. At this point, Step 6, it became necessary to consult professionals and professional literature in order to determine what inputs would best facilitate the production of the outputs identified in Step 5. Did the Big/Little systems need individual counseling by a trained professional or would specially designed activities result in the desired ends? What was the most practical alternative, given the available resources? It was decided that a self-instructional, multimedia program would be the most feasible mode for inputting information to the Big. It was hypothesized that, with the proper information, the Big would change the processes occurring in the Big/Little system and output a Little capable of appropriate interaction with the self and other systems. This information was viewed as one of the needs of the Big/Little systems. All of the Big/Little pairings would not need the information available, but given the needs assessment data, the areas identified as most critical to the largest number of systems would be considered.

In this particular example, the needs identified as a result of the application of the needs assessment strategy were consistent with those initially suggested by the administrator of the supra- or parent system but considerably more specific and detailed. In addition, the needs resulting from the assessment strategy were based upon a conceptual framework that permitted the gathering of logically consistent data, as opposed to being based on intuition.

The example given involves a small number of two-person systems in which behavioral interactions were of paramount importance, but the needs assessment strategy is applicable to other situations where the systems contain large numbers of individuals and something other than behavioral repertoires are the target outputs.

SUMMARY

The behavioral systems model provides a conceptual framework upon which a needs assessment strategy can be based. The strategy suggested here relies on the premise that most behavioral systems are open; that is, they receive inputs and produce outputs that flow to other receiving systems. The desired effect of outputs on the receiving systems dictates what the outputs should be and what is needed by *the system* in order to produce the proper outputs. Given this position, an adequate needs assessment strategy should result in an identification of the problems with the receiving systems of that system and an identification of the inputs necessary to remedy the problems.

The six-step procedure suggested contains two paths that are differentiated on the basis of whether or not the system in question has goals. In either case, the assessment of needs is predicated upon the relationship of a system to its receiving systems and to the attainment of certain desired conditions in those receiving systems.

The methods used and the conceptual analysis completed in the Big Brother/Sister program were very similar to what can be done with any behavioral system that can be identified with reasonable accuracy. The strategy presented is applicable to a wide variety of current programs and problems and provides a general methodological approach for behavior management specialists.

CHAPTER SEVEN: GUIDELINES
FOR PRACTICAL APPLICATION

Guideline 7.1: Expect that the operation of most systems will not be based on the type of needs assessment described in Chapter 7. This deficiency will not prevent you from implementing successful behavior management programs, but it may lead you to question the wisdom of those responsible for the operation of the system.

— *Expect to find systems in which a preference for a certain process (regardless of outcome or needs) may result in needs of the receiving system being aggravated rather than lessened. You may be asked to apply your behavior management skills to facilitate the process, again, regardless of needs or outcome.*
— *Unfortunately, the ethics of behavior management do not include mention of needs assessment as a precursor to intervention; therefore, nearsighted good intentions will often substitute for reasoned foresight.*
— *Integrity may be the characteristic that helps a behavior manager refuse to participate in a program that will worsen rather than alleviate the problems in the receiving systems.*

Guideline 7.2: When evaluating a system, keep in mind that needs are often dynamic; therefore, conditions once existing may no longer be present. The system you are evaluating may be based upon the results of a needs assessment that is no longer applicable.

Guideline 7.3: When planning or designing a system, keep in mind that the actions and decisions in the flowchart (Figure 7.2) depicting the needs assessment strategy were selected for generality and broad application. You would be wise to follow the general intent of that flowchart and to devise your own specific steps in a sequence that proves effective for you and your situation.

Neither the concept of needs nor the tasks and purposes of needs assessment should change when you devise your own assessment strategy. Don't alter your destination; simply stay flexible about how you get there.

EIGHT
ANALYSIS OF
BEHAVIORAL SYSTEMS

The purpose of the first seven chapters of this book has been to describe a conceptual framework that behavior management specialists can use to obtain a broad view of the situation in which individual behavior is to be managed. The argument has been made that a broad view can help to alleviate the problems in managing behavior that can arise from *the system* in which the individual operates rather than from the idividual.

Because behavior management specialists encounter and create systems with a wide variety of structures and functions, it is most advantageous to provide system concepts as basic tools and to encourage the user to implement them in whatever fashion seems most useful. It would be a mistake to try to convince behavior managers that only a complete system analysis is functional. To the contrary, it may be beneficial for a certain behavior manager to identify a single component of a specific system in order to improve a behavior management program.

Similarly, the way one goes about understanding a system can vary from system to system and from one behavior manager to another. With this in mind, the following description of system analysis procedures is presented only as an example of what a reasonably complete system analysis would contain. A system analysis outline is presented in Appendix A for those readers who may have need for a concise itemization of the steps in such a procedure.

DEVELOP A PRELIMINARY
DESCRIPTION OF THE SYSTEM

- Identify the general boundaries.
- Identify the general processes that are operating.
- Determine the general function of the system.

The information needed for a preliminary description of the system can usually be obtained from documents such as the program proposal, the annual report, or the administrative policies and procedures manual. In addition, most administrative personnel can provide the basic information that is needed. The questions to be asked by the behavior manager/system analyst in one form or another are:

- With whom or what do you work?
- Where and how do you begin working with them?
- When and how do you decide that you are through working with them?
- What do you do with them?
- Why do you do what you do?

Example: Three dentists from a small midwestern community had returned from a dental conference in which a topic of discussion had been staff management and morale. All three recognized symptoms of poor staff management practices existing in their individual offices and decided to engage a faculty member from the local college to help them resolve their alleged problems. Elizabeth Thompson, who taught counseling and planned-change courses, was highly recommended by several members of the Kiwanis Club. Thompson met with the three dentists and discussed their situations. The perceived problems, as described by the dentists, were vague and not very focused, but Thompson was able to discern that some of the complaints involved patient management (missed appointments, delinquent accounts, and poor home care) while other complaints had more to do with the staff ("bad" attitudes, poor morale, lack of professional interest, and "ignorance about the realities of running an office"). Thompson thought that she could set up the six seminar sessions that the dentists requested but that she could best help them if she better understood each dental office as a system. A quick system analysis was in order.

Thompson spoke with the staff of each office for an hour or so and began her analysis with the development of a preliminary description. In all three offices, the system boundaries very seldom extended beyond the physical confines of their respective offices. Although one dentist had, on occasion, been called to the emergency room of the hospital, such extensions of system boundaries were usually delegated to the oral surgeon in the commuinty. Two offices performed general dental procedures with adults and children while the third specialized in periodontal care and only saw patients with some degree of gum disease. The two major thrusts of all offices were prevention and remediation of dental disease.

ANALYZE SYSTEM GOALS

- Identify design goals (if they exist).
- Identify goals that are currently operating (if any).

Design goals are the original goal statements of the system. If they exist, they are often found in the charter, design document, or administrative manual of the organization. The designer or originator of the system is often knowledgeable of the original goals. It is not unusual for the system to be operating with statements that are incorrectly focused, vague, or without a time dimension and, therefore, without goals from the behavior management specialist's perspective. However, these statements will be called goals by organization members. Behavior managers would be wise to simply acknowledge the difference in definitions and turn their attention to identifying possible goals that were not part of the original design but that have been adopted since for current use.

Example: Although all three dental offices certainly had direction, only one had goals, in the behavioral system sense. The periodontist had worked out a plan with his accountant that included the goal of "taking home 8 percent more income from the practice this year than last." Thompson was pleasantly surprised when she realized that all four conditions for a goal were met: (1) the periodontist was the receiving system, (2) the change in his state was specific (an 8 percent increase in income), (3) it would occur within a specified time dimension, and (4) it was manifest (the receptionist and the assistant were aware of it).

SCOPE IN THE SYSTEM

- Identify the location and structure of the input and output boundaries.
- Identify the special conditions operating at the input and output boundaries.

Information about input and output boundary structure and location can usually be secured from administrative policy and procedure documents as well as from management personnel. Observation of suspected boundaries will also provide data that should help to identify the places where inputs get into the system and how they get into the system. Of course, some potential outputs will not be permitted to leave the system. The restrictive conditions that prevent potential inputs and outputs from entering or leaving the system are the boundary conditions of the system.

Example: Thompson already had an accurate idea of the boundaries of each system by having developed a preliminary description of each of the offices. At this time she discovered some interesting boundary conditions. For example, one office would not take Medicaid or Medicare patients, all three had a list of patients who were referred elsewhere because of chronic delinquent accounts, and of course, the periodontist limited his practice to those patients having gum problems. The two general practice dentists did not grant emergency appointments unless the person requesting the appointment was an established patient and injury or trauma had occurred. On the output side, patients were not encouraged to leave the office until clinical procedures were completed, that is, fillings were trimmed and polished, x-rays were completed, and the effects of anesthesia had dissipated. Of course, patient files were not permitted to leave the office, and salary checks were outputted on a regular schedule.

SPECIFYING THE OUTPUT ENSEMBLE

- Identify output types.
- Determine output rate by type.
- Identify nonselected outputs.

There are a number of sources of information about outputs—system records, the decider, the personnel working on the output boundary, and one's own observations. It is not unusual for behavioral systems to output at variable rates so one should not expect a steady output level over time. One may have to actually observe or communicate with the receiving system to know which outputs are accepted and processed as opposed to those that may be turned away, examined and destroyed, or placed in storage indefinitely. All of these latter responses amount to nonselection of outputs.

Example: Thompson believed that it was not necessary to have a detailed, quantitative account of the output ensemble of each office and that a general overview would suffice. The two general practice offices output-ted more adult patients than children, and all patients leaving the offices had received some degree of preparation for home care or preventive measures. In terms of corrective treatment, more patients left these two offices with filled teeth than with any other corrective outcome. Patients were often referred to other offices for oral surgery (wisdom teeth) or orthodontic treatment. All patients from all three offices had their teeth cleaned by dental hygienists, if necessary. It was interesting to discover that the major output from the periodontist's system was a patient who had been thoroughly examined, had had teeth cleaned, and had been instructed in proper therapeutic home care of teeth and gums. In all three offices, the most common nonselected output was instruction in home care and proper diet. Many patients did not floss their teeth nor did they restrict decay-producing foods from their diets. Often, six-month recalls for checkups were also nonselected outputs.

IDENTIFY TARGETS

- Identify inferred receiving systems (targets),
  —when goals exist.
  —in the absence of goals.
- Develop specifications of the inferred receiving systems.
  —Identify state variables.
  —Identify the values of state variables.

When goals exist and outputs flow to a system other than the intended receiving system, one can infer that the system actually receiving the outputs is a target. Likewise, when goals do not exist, the systems to which outputs flow are also targets. The output ensemble information provided above is the basis for inferring that certain receiving systems and, hence, certain targets, do exist. By observing the nature of the outputs, the output rate, and the effect of the outputs on the inferred receiving system, one can begin to identify which target system states are influenced and to what extent.

Example: The two primary targets that Thompson identified in each of the three dental offices involved the dentists themselves and their respective sets of patients. Each office outputted money to the dentist on a regular basis. The amount outputted varied according to the amount of money inputted to the system. For the two dentists who did not have goals, the value desired for the variable "dentist's income" was vague and not shared with the entire office staff. Thompson finally described this target as "a continuous increase in the dentist's income, influenced by the needs of the dentist's family at that particular time." (The contrast between this ill-defined target and the periodontist's goal of an 8 percent increase was remarkable to Thompson.)

The patient-related target was vague, not manifest, and without a time dimension. It generally involved the dental health of the set of patients in each office. Thompson was able to state it this way: "Patients will be free of oral or dental disease and maintain that condition."

Other less prominent targets existed for each of the systems, but the only one that Thompson pursued to any extent had to do with the incomes of the various staff members. It appeared to her that these targets could be described as "a staff member's income will be as low as possible, yet high enough to maintain the staff member's state of employment."

DEVELOP INPUT ENSEMBLE SPECIFICATIONS

- Identify output type.
- Identify output rate by type.
- Identify input source systems.

The gathering of information about inputs is straightforward and usually is accomplished easily from within the system. The important questions to be answered are:

- What comes into the system?
- How often do these inputs enter the system?
- Where do they come from?

Example: Thompson found that patient inputs directly corresponded to outputs (as one would expect!). However, the rate of input varied according to the time of day and the school calendar. Adult male patients were seen most often late in the afternoon, and the entire patient load decreased during summer months.

Income to the system varied with patient load and with efforts to reduce accounts receivable. However, Thompson noted at this time that an inverse relationship seemed to exist between patient load and efforts to collect outstanding bills. If more patients were seen each day, the receptionist had less time to spend on accounts receivable than if fewer patients appeared.

DESCRIBE THE EXTERNAL NETWORK

- Describe the arrangement of input source systems.
- Describe the arrangement of first order receiving systems—
  —those related to goals.
  —those related to targets.
- Identify second, third, and higher order receiving systems.
- Identify critical intervening systems.
  —Describe the function of the invervening systems.
  —Describe the process used by the intervening systems.
  —Identify the contingencies impinging on the intervening systems.
- Identify the suprasystem arrangement for the system under examination.

Having previously identified goal-related and target-related receiving systems and input source systems, one can now put them together with the system to form the network of systems outside the boundaries of the system being analyzed. Some of the questions to be answered at this point are:

- How are the input source systems arranged?
- In what sequence do outputs flow through first and higher order receiving systems?
- Where the does the flow end?
- Which systems intervene in the output flow?
- What purpose do the intervening systems serve?
- How do the intervening systems accomplish their purposes?
- What are the contingencies on intervening system performance?
- Who controls the contingencies?
- If the system being analyzed is part of a hierarchy, what is the supra-system?

Example: Thompson found that much of the external network for each system had already been identified. Patients were both the signal being processed by the system and one of the first order receiving systems. In fact, in the network associated with the patient-related target, there was nothing beyond the patient that was significant.

A very important second order receiving system in the network associated with the "dentist's income" target was the dentist's family. Expenses incurred by the family established financial needs that the dentist was supposed to meet by receiving money from the dental practice. Since one dentist was supporting his elderly mother-in-law in a costly nursing home (third order receiving system), considerable pressure was placed upon the family (second order receiving system), the dentist (first order receiving system), and hence the dental office (the system).

Insurance companies were identified as important systems that closed the input-output loop and converted a bill for services (output) to the patient (first order receiving system) into a payment for services (input) from the insurance company (second order receiving system) to the dental office (which in this case became the third order receiving system). From the dentist's perspective, there were no contingencies that could be placed upon insurance companies to increase the likelihood of prompt, accurate payments.

None of the three offices were part of a larger practice or clinic, so suprasystem analysis was not necessary.

DESCRIBE THE PROCESS

- Identify components.
- Identify and describe subsystems.
  —Identify subsystem inputs and outputs.

—Identify subsystem networks.
- Identify the time required for process.
- Describe behavioral subsystems.
  —Develop flowcharts.
  —Identify flow at various levels of detail (see Appendix A).
- Develop behavioral descriptions.
  —Identify reinforcers.
  —Identify discriminative stimuli.
  —Identify contingencies.

Observation is often the most effective method for determining what processes are carried out in the system, although the decider can sometimes describe the basic aspects of process such as components, subsystems, and process time. It is important to keep in mind that administrative or managerial structures may not coincide with process or subsystem structures. Furthermore, processes may partially overlap, and individuals may be components of more than one subsystem. When identifying process, one often asks the question, "What do you do next (after you did that)?" There are, of course, many other questions to which you will seek answers:

Components:

- Who does that?
- Does the same person do that and *that*?
- Who else would be involved in a situation like that?

Subsystems:

- If this (input) is first seen at this point, where is it last seen (output)?
- What other inputs come in at this point?
- What are the other inputs that might be handled in other ways by other people?
- Do you ever output anything like this?

Process Time:

- How long does it usually take to do that?

Behavioral Subsystems:

- If the decision at this point is "Yes (No)," what happens next?
- You have said that X occurs here and Y happens next—are you sure that nothing takes place between X and Y?

Example: Thompson was quite aware of the lengthy time and abundant resources necessary to do a complete analysis of subsystems and processes. Although she was quite sure that this part of each dental office was a potential problem area, she felt that an extensive analysis was not appropriate. Accordingly, she tried to get a general picture without undue attention to details. She had already identified the four components of each system: dentist, dental hygienist, assistant, and receptionist. The staff members tended to see each office broken down into subsystems that corresponded to the positions in the office, that is, a dentist subsystem, a hygienist subsystem, and so on. Thompson, however, perceived the subsystems as cutting across these positions and relating more to functions in the office than to people. The four major subsystems that she finally identified were treatment, office management, education, and equipment maintenance. She further subdivided each subsystem into operations.

Subsystem: Treatment
   Operations: Examination of patient
                   Diagnosis and planning
                   Case presentation
                   Clinical procedures (dentist)
                   Prophylaxis (primarily hygienist)
                   Laboratory procedures
                   Operatory preparation
Subsystem: Office Management
   Operations: File/records management
                   Billing and collecting
                   Appointments
                   Equipment and supplies inventory
                   Physical environment upkeep
                   Coordination of office functions
                   Patient recall
                   Personnel management
                         Hiring
                         Promotion
                         Leave
                         Firing
Subsystem: Education
   Operations: Case presentation
                   Oral hygiene instruction
                   Public service
                   Patient behavior management
Subsystem: Equipment Maintenance
   Operations: Cleaning (instruments and equipment)
                   Instrument sterilization
                   Instrument sharpening
                   Replacement of equipment and instruments
                   Laundry
                   Lubrication

Thompson pursued some of the operations down to specific behavioral levels because she realized that this was at the heart of the dentists' original complaints. Staff members were performing their duties, but it wasn't very clear as to what their duties were. It also became apparent that the signals or discriminative stimuli for certain behaviors were unclear and variable; hence, even if one knew what to do, it was not always obvious when to do it. None of the three offices used praise or any other type of attempted reinforcement for appropriate behavior (other than on a highly intermittent, nonspecific schedule).

DESCRIBE PROCESS FEEDBACK MECHANISMS

- Describe the sensor(s).
- Describe the nature of the feedback.
- Identify the feedback interval.

The best source of information about feedback mechanisms is the system decider. However, a system may have several individuals performing the decider function, so each should be queried about the process information received. Once a possible feedback mechanism is identified, observation of its operation may be the best means for further analysis. Questions that may be pursued include:

- How do you (system decider) get the information about process?
- What information do you receive about processes taking place?
- How often do you get the information?
- Is the information usually accurate?
- What would you do if you got X information about process?

Example: Thompson had begun to realize that the three offices operated with a laissez-faire style of management. This meant that the dentist was not the major decider in the system, but rather, each staff member was left to make many administrative decisions. Those decisions and actions that were guided by policy were seldom observed, so the dentist received little if any feedback regarding the carrying out of processes (other than his own) within the office. Although one dentist was displeased with the work of his assistant, it was because of the consequences of inappropriate actions (and not the actions themselves) that he was aware of the problem.

DESCRIBE OUTPUT FEEDBACK MECHANISMS

- Describe the sensor(s).
- Describe the nature of the feedback.
- Identify the feedback interval.
- Identify the desired performance level.

Once again, the system decider is the best source of information about output feedback. Some of the questions to be asked are:

- How do you know how many of those things leave the system?
- How do you know whether or not it is good enough to send out?
- How often do you get information about X?
- Is the information usually accurate?
- What would you do if you got Z information about output?

Example: It became apparent to Thompson that the dentists probably served as the decider, process component, and output feedback mechanism for clinical treatment, that is, each dentist decided what clinical procedure should be done, carried out that procedure, and monitored the outcomes of the procedure. Furthermore, after the hygienist cleaned a patient's teeth, the dentist examined the patient; therefore, if the quality of patient-related outputs varied, the dentist would know. This was not true of most of the paperwork and telephone calls that left the office; no one monitored output to determine rate or quality. Thompson began to think that laissez-faire management in this regard included the absence of any feedback mechanism monitoring outputs from the system.

DESCRIBE ENVIRONMENTAL
FEEDBACK MECHANISMS

- Identify feedback related to goals.
  —Describe the sensor.
  —Describe the nature of the feedback.
  —Identify the feedback interval.
- Identify feedback related to targets.
  —Describe the feedback type.
  —Identify the feedback interval.
  —Describe the feedback channel.
  —Identify the relationship of feedback to system values.

Some of the important questions to ask, in one form or another, are:

- How does information about the receiving system get back to the system?
- What is the nature of the information you get about the receiving system?
- How does the information you get relate to system goals?
- How often does the information come to you?
- Is the information reliable?
- What would you do if feedback said the receiving system was in State A instead of State B, as you desired?

Example: Thompson knew that, for two offices, environmental feedback would have to come from targets. It seemed remarkable to her that the two dentists with vague income targets got very little accurate information about the state of their income. It was even more interesting for her to discover that patients were the sensors for monitoring the states of their dental health. Only in the case of extractions did one dentist telephone patients within 24 hours following the surgery to inquire about their condition. Otherwise, there seemed to be no regular, structured environmental feedback mechanisms.

The periodontist, on the other hand, received monthly reports from his accountant that showed the net income for the past month and the amount projected as necessary in order to achieve the goal of an 8 percent increase. Unfortunately, the same type of feedback mechanism had not been devised to monitor the states of his patients' dental health.

IDENTIFY CONSTRAINTS ON THE SYSTEM

- Identify resource constraints—economic, manpower, and technological.
- Identify administrative constraints—philosophical, political, policy, procedural, and social.

The identification of system constraints generally requires "why" questions, and almost any component of the system will be a source of information as to why something does or does not exist within the system. Keep in mind that constraints may restrict the function of a system even if they are imagined or invalid. In addition, the constraints that operate at the system level may impact at the level of the individual and, hence, influence behavior management attempts. Awareness of the constraints on a system will often allow the behavior management specialist to avoid system problems when behavior management programs are initiated.

Example: The two important constraints that Thompson detected in all three dental offices fell into the resource and administrative categories. The resource constraint limited the time and energy that the dentist could devote to managerial activities. His time was primarily taken up with clinical procedures and other types of interaction with patients. Furthermore, on the administrative/philosophical side, none of the three dentists expressed an interest in performing the management functions. By and large, they wanted the offices to run by themselves, and as one said, "I don't want to have to reward and motivate my staff to do things— that's their job, that's what they get paid for."

Another less well-defined resource constraint involved the availability of inputs. According to the dentists, three factors were limiting their number of patients. The first factor was the large number of dentists in the community, which meant fewer patients for each office. The second factor was the high-inflation, high-unemployment economy that influenced people to use their limited purchasing power on something other than "elective dental treatment." Finally, the success of preventive dental health programs had operated as a factor to reduce the number of people needing professional dental care. Thus, the offices could not easily increase their productivity by taking on more patients; patients were not always available.

FINAL ACTIONS AND
RECOMMENDATIONS IN THE EXAMPLE

As a result of the perspective gained from the system analysis, Thompson made recommendations that she would not have made prior to the analysis. The problems originally identified by the dentists could probably have been resolved by simple behavior management approaches while ignoring the offices as systems, but the process would be more effective if system characteristics were considered. Initially, Thompson had in mind defining the problem areas behaviorally, collecting baselines on the problem behaviors, and suggesting contingencies that would reduce the frequency of undesirable behaviors and increase the incidence of desirable behaviors. Once the systems information was available, however, she decided that conflicts were certain to arise and that other steps might also be appropriate. The following is a brief description of her actions and recommendations.

• In light of the minimal internal network information, Thompson set up workshop sessions for each office at which she had each staff member identify the actions performed and decisions made most frequently. In addition, if possible, the staff member listed the criteria used to make the decision or the discriminative stimuli that signaled an action. This information not only provided an identification of which behaviors possibly needed management and who was responsible for the action but also provided the skeleton for an office manual and helped the staff to detect the conflicts in assignments and bottlenecks that reduced efficiency.
• At another workshop session, Thompson had the staff identify those behaviors and decisions that were most critical to system functioning but which were also difficult, aversive to perform, or in conflict with other behaviors. Not surprisingly, these corresponded quite highly with the problem areas initially identified by the dentists. Thompson explained the concepts of positive reinforcement, extinction, and intermittent reinforcement to maintain behavior. She also anticipated the

dentists' questions about professional responsibility, duty, attitudes, and self-direction (which were all offered as reasons for not having to actually manage the behavior of the office staff). Having established that some form of management might be necessary, she terminated that session with the question, "How does one reinforce behavior if there isn't any time to observe the behavior taking place?" (That pretty much summed up the dentists' situation.)

• Considering the constraints on the systems, at the next session Thompson suggested methods for managing behavior without observing the actual responses, such as monitoring permanent products of the behavior or utilizing self-reporting in the form of checklists. She also identified the usefulness of checklists for prompting appropriate behavior and gaining process feedback. Each staff put together appropriate checklists that could be used intermittently to support behavior patterns. The formulation of the checklists further solidified the policies and procedures that should appear in the respective office manuals.

• The system targets that Thompson perceived would continue to hinder evaluation and control, so she next discussed the utility of goals with the dentists. She elaborated on their functions of evaluation and control of the system. Fortunately, she had the periodontist's goal to use as an example. The development of goals was a strange and uncomfortable exercise for the dentists, but they pursued it diligently (perhaps because Thompson had assured them that she would put no pressure on them to adopt the goals they were developing, the decision to do so would be entirely up to the dentists).

• By using the periodontist's goal as an example, she was able to show how regular, accurate environmental feedback allowed for evaluation of progress and control over system activities. In addition, she convinced the periodontist of the value in using income over 8 percent as monetary reinforcement for appropriate behaviors on the part of the staff. She assured them all that regular use of praise would probably be effective as a reinforcer, but if the staff was willing to make extra efforts to exceed the 8 percent income level, she asked, "Why shouldn't they be reinforced in the form of bonuses?" If her inference about the "staff income target" was correct, the staff members were probably in a deprived financial state and attempted monetary reinforcers would probably be very effective.

• It was easy to generalize office goal setting to patient goal setting and reinforcement of appropriate patient behaviors. The dentists and their staff members readily grasped the applicability of positive reinforcement to patient home care, but they were not certain that they wished to take on that responsibility. Thompson pointed out the compatibility between the "dental health targets" of the offices and the use of behavior management techniques. The periodontist and one of the general practitioners adopted a procedure of patient goal setting in terms of dental health and arranged for tangible positive consequences for achievement of subgoals. These two offices then had environmental feedback mechanisms that allowed for evaluation of progress toward individual dental health goals.

• Having completed the foregoing steps, Thompson could then focus on solutions to specific behavior problems. Since most of the important staff behaviors (in relation to goals and targets) were already defined, it was a simple matter to collect baseline data. The results of the baseline phase indicated that the receptionist in the periodontist's office had high rates of missed or incomplete responses (not incorrect responses), whereas the assistant in one of the general practice offices responded incorrectly more often than was appropriate. Thompson had a hunch that the receptionist simply needed regularly occurring discriminative stimuli to signal that certain behaviors should occur. A special checklist was devised for the receptionist, which the periodontist examined at the end of each workday. The following contingency was established: if the receptionist completed the checklist by 5:00 P.M. on seven of eight consecutive days, the staff would have lunch at the local restaurant on the ninth day. (This meant that about every two weeks the dentist would take his staff to lunch.)

The assistant with the high incorrect behavior rates was another problem altogether. The fact that she performed appropriately at times indicated that she at least knew what to do. The existing, highly intermittent schedules of reinforcement just did not seem sufficient to maintain her behavior. A simple checklist was set up for her, but she "forgot" to use it about 50 percent of the time. Regular praise from the dentist, contingent upon the presentation of a completed checklist, increased completion rates to about 88 percent, but after three weeks the assistant appeared to be satiating on praise and the dentist was "forgetting" to examine the checklist. About this time Thompson explained the contingency and positive results from the periodontist's office to the dentist. A similar contingency was set up for the behavior of the assistant in the general practice office, and for the first two weeks the assistant's behavior rate was 100 percent correct. Thompson's regular involvement with the offices ended at that time.

• Four months later, Thompson did a brief follow-up on the offices. The periodontist had instituted a profit-sharing plan for income in excess of 8 percent. His accountant provided feedback, which was graphed and posted, to the staff every two weeks. The receptionist still used the checklist intermittently and the staff still had "lunch out" every two weeks if things "ran smoothly." Profits were increasing, and the office was operating more efficiently and effectively than ever.

The office with the malfunctioning assistant was in a shambles. From what Thompson could detect from an interview or two, it seemed that the dentist had put off "lunch out" (reinforcement) even though the assistant's behavior rates were initially appropriate. As the assistant reverted back to her high rates of incorrect behavior, the receptionist began to express her sentiments about having to do "someone else's job" and "not being treated to lunch on top of it." The dentist had examined the accounts receivable list and suggested that the receptionist was not doing her job at collecting. He called the staff together and informed them that "everyone would have to tighten their belts and work a little harder and better. The office was not producing like it could or should. It was too bad that the consultant had not helped them at all." The following week the dentist's wife was overheard in the grocery store describing to a friend the new home in the "exclusive" neighborhood that they were considering.

The remaining general practice office was progressing nicely. Several things were happening: an office manual that clearly identified policies was being typed; the staff was meeting regularly to discuss office goals, policies, and responsibilities; the dentist was liberally using praise and gift certificates as reinforcers for appropriate behavior (and especially for emergency overtime and shortened lunch hours); and the dentist had informed the staff that, as soon as profits reached a certain level (that he and his accountant would identify shortly), a profit-sharing plan would be established.

Thompson's comment to herself on the way back to campus was, "Two outta three ain't bad."

The preceding discussion was only meant to provide examples of questions to be answered and possible sources of information. Interaction with different systems will require different approaches. The examples of questions were stated in systems jargon, but the use of such a specialized language is not advisable when attempting to communicate with persons not familiar with systems concepts. Learning the language of the individuals in the system and translating information to fit into the behavioral system framework are skills that will prove invaluable to the behavior manager who wishes to understand the organizational context in which behavior management will occur.

CHAPTER EIGHT: GUIDELINES
FOR PRACTICAL APPLICATION

Guideline 8.1: *When called upon for a specific behavior management task, remember that the behavioral system framework was meant to be basically conceptual in nature so that you could quickly and easily see the "big picture." The individual concepts are consistent with the whole framework, but each is also applicable in its own right. Use the parts that are relevant to the task at hand. A full-blown system analysis may consume time that could be better spent collecting baseline behavior rates.*

On the other hand, if extensive behavior change is indicated or if program evaluation is to be carried out, the complete analysis procedure, based on the behavioral system framework, will help immensely.

Guideline 8.2: At whatever level of analysis you are working be careful to avoid "free association" analysis, in which the answer to one question stimulates another question whose answer makes you think of yet another question, and so on. You may get some exciting (and stimulating) information this way, but the conceptual image of the system that you develop is often fragmented and disjointed. It is better to use the analysis outline and to gather information in an orderly, structured fashion.

Guideline 8.3: Keep in mind that your image of the system will grow as you gather new information. As parts are added, you may have to loop back to previous analysis sections and probe the area again with different questions from those used the last time. In that sense, systems analysis is an orderly, iterative process that eventually results in a relatively complete perception of the system.

How do you know when to stop cycling through the system? Try stating things about the system in your own words. If system members do not make additions to your statements or correct you, try observing the system for a period of time. If you do not see anything that is different from your image of the system and you can predict system activity accurately, you probably have a reasonably complete analysis.

Guideline 8.4: One of the most difficult requirements to meet when analyzing a system is that of being conceptually flexible enough to accept new notions about the system. Once you begin to see a system in a certain way (suppose it appears to have two distinct subsystems), you will find it increasingly difficult to alter that perception (for example, recognizing that the two apparent subsystems are actually carrying out the same process and, therefore, are only one subsystem). The image that you build of the system should be consistent with observations that you (and others) make of the system in action. In the event of inconsistency, consider ideas about the system that are different from yours—the more radically different, the better. Be patient—hear them out—then rebuild your image of the system, incorporating notions that are consistent with the system observation data.

— *Invariably, targets present the most vexing instance of the problem of inflexibility for the system analyst. Once you realize a direction in which the system is going, it is often difficult to consider other directions. Try to remember that a system may be proceeding toward several states for itself and its members* and *toward certain states for its receiving systems.*

— With regard to the problem of identifying targets, keep in mind that the major question may not be whether or not the system is actually pursuing a direction but rather how vigorously the system seems to be moving toward that target. The priority of a target may have a much greater impact on system activity (inputs, process, outputs) than will the simple existence of the target.

NINE
PLANNING AND DESIGNING
A BEHAVIORAL SYSTEM

Planning and designing a *new* system requires application of the behavioral system framework in different ways from that required for system analysis. Obviously, in analysis the system already exists and your task is to determine how it functions, whereas with planning and designing a system, the need may already be there but the system is not. As a result, not only do the steps taken to plan a system require some creative efforts by the planner, but also the sequence or flow through the various parts of the behavior systems model is different in planning from what it is in analysis. The discussion that follows can be used as a general guide when preparing a grant proposal, adding a program to a previously functioning program, or in any other situation in which a system must be created. As with the system analysis outline, the outline for designing a system is not meant to portray a rigidly prescribed procedure, although the developmental logic does suggest that certain steps be done in sequence. (A concise outline of the system planning and design procedure can be found in Appendix B.) In a sense, the planning and design sequence flows backward, that is, from the receiving system to the system and then to the input source systems. In the behavioral system model in Figure 2.1, this backward progression begins with needs assessment of the receiving system and progresses back to the system inputs.

- Identify the receiving systems.
- Identify the state variables to be changed in the receiving systems.
- Identify the current and desired values of the state variables.
- Identify the inputs (to the receiving systems) needed to move state variables from current to desired values.

Needs assessment concentrates on the identification of what is desired in the receiving system(s). Note that the needs assessment is not completed for the system to be created but rather for the receiving systems to which the prospective system will output. Receiving system conditions have been called *state variables,* and it is important to determine what condition the system is currently in (State 1) and what the desired condition is (State 2). The prospective system will have as a purpose to move its receiving system(s) from State 1 to State 2. Once it is known where the receiving system is at present and where it is desired that it be, the task of deciding what it needs to attain the desired condition can be completed.

Example: By a not-so-strange twist of fate, Lawrence Adams and Elizabeth Thompson teamed up as consultants on a project for Southern States Industrial Chemicals Company (SSICC). SSICC was the product of a merger between a small chemical plant and a very successful distributor of industrial cleaning products. The merger had not been managed well, and the president of SSICC retained Adams and Thompson (who were now partners in Behavioral Business Systems, Inc.) to design and assist in the implementation of a program that would resolve some of the problems, especially in the marketing department. Adams and Thompson agreed that the behavior management approach was probably appropriate in this case and that the behavioral systems approach would be useful for planning the program.

Thompson handled the needs assessment stage. She purposely left the structure and location of the proposed system (program) vague so as not to be influenced by preconceived notions of process. She obviously wanted to focus on outcomes. The receiving systems to which the prospective system would output were the marketing and sales components of the organizational entity called the "marketing department." In some cases the receiving systems would be individual sales representatives or marketing personnel and at other times the entire "marketing system" would receive inputs. Identifying the state variables to be changed in the receiving systems was a difficult problem because the president of SSICC was not certain about the nature of the problem that he wished to have resolved. After several sessions with the president, Thompson was able to identify the following state variables as exemplifying the problem:

1. Turnover in sales personnel; only 36 percent of the sales staff remained with the company longer than three years.
2. Morale of both marketing and sales personnel; this variable could be evaluated through the assessment of absenteeism and numbers of employees late for work. In addition, the director of the marketing depart-

ment could subjectively evaluate the quantity and quality of complaints at "group discussion" sessions.

3. Incidence of stress-related health problems; the company physician pointed out that the occurrence of migraine headaches, ulcers, high blood pressure, and other stress-related problems among the marketing department employees was higher than in any other department.

4. Productivity in the form of orders placed with SSICC.

Company records revealed the *current values* of each state variable except for quantity and quality of complaints at "group discussion" sessions. Since these sessions may have been reinforcing events in themselves, Thompson decided not to recommend initiating them simply to attain a baseline.

The *desired values* of each state variable were as follows:

1. Turnover—no greater than 40 percent after three years
2. Absenteeism—no greater than the company average
3. Tardiness for work—no greater than the company average
4. Quantity and quality of complaints—"serious" complaints reduced to zero; total complaints reduced by 75 percent
5. Stress-related health problems—no greater than the company average
6. Orders placed with SSICC—a 15 percent increase

Thompson and Adams spent many hours working out the various inputs that would effect the desired changes in the identified state variables. They finally settled on the following:

1. A graduated schedule of salary and vacation increases for staying with SSICC
2. A schedule of bonuses for reduced absenteeism and tardiness for work
3. Weekly feedback on absenteeism and tardiness-for-work rates
4. A program of stress assessment and stress reduction to reduce stress-related health problems
5. A plan for monitoring and reinforcing sales representatives to secure orders and perform the appropriate behavioral approximations (calls, interviews, new contacts, and so forth)

ASSESS CONSTRAINTS

- Identify resource and administrative constraints that would influence achievement of desired values of the receiving system state variables.
- Identify resource and administrative constraints that would influence necessary inputs to the receiving system.

Resource (economic, manpower, technological) or administrative (philosophical, political, policy, procedural, social) constraints often will prohibit the attainment of the desired condition (State 2) and/or the necessary inputs. The feasibility of the prospective system attaining its goals is to be seriously questioned if important constraints exist. This is a point at which it is important to consider not only the obvious constraining variables such as budget and available technology, but also the interactive effects between state variables that may cause unintended changes. If changing Variable A from State 1 to State 2 means that Variable B will inevitably be changed to an undesirable state, this may be a constraint that will prevent any change at all. Figure 9.1 illustrates the focus of the analysis of constraints.

Example: Even before Thompson had completed the needs assessment, Adams had identified two constraints that would seriously limit the outcomes the proposed program could hope to achieve. The first was a policy constraint that would limit the use of monetary reinforcers; wages and salaries at SSICC were rigidly set (even in the absence of a union), and upper management would not consent to revisions for the purposes of this project. Secondly, this project was not given highest priority, and hence, the budget would not support the effort that Thompson and Adams would have to put forth to achieve the desired changes in the values of the identified state variables. A less certain constraint could result from the interaction of achieving stress reductions and the subsequent effect on production; no one was sure that the former would not act to reduce the latter. Although not explicit, a fourth constraint was also possible—the program might have to be implemented through existing resources of the company.

DEVELOP GOALS

- Estimate the amount of time required to achieve each of the desired values of the receiving system state variables.
- Compile the desired values of receiving system state variables, with the estimates of time required for achievement.
- Compare the compiled statements (goals) with the constraints identified earlier.

With the description of the desired conditions and the estimates of the time required to meet those conditions, it is possible to generate goal statements and to compare them to the restrictions imposed by resource and administrative constraints. If the feasibility of attaining the goals is

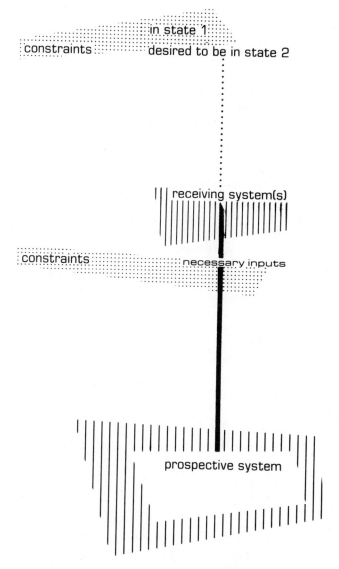

FIGURE 9.1   System design after completion of item
2 of the design outline.

reduced markedly by constraints, goals should either be revised or a
decision to not develop the prospective system should be made.

Example: Thompson and Adams reasoned that the previously identified
constraints would prevent the occurrence of several of the necessary
inputs that had been identified. Therefore, from their perspective, several
possible goals were eliminated from consideration. The president of

SSICC agreed with their assessment and accepted a limited package of goals for the proposed program. Here are the goals that Adams and Thompson developed:

Goal No. 1: Within 18 months of the initiation of a stress management program, the stress-related health problems of the sales and marketing staff would be no greater than the company average.

Goal No. 2: Within ten months of the initiation of a management program, absenteeism and tardiness of sales and marketing staff would decrease by 9 percent from baseline figures.

Although not stated in the form of a goal, it was agreed that turnover and productivity rates should not increase or decrease, respectively, from baseline levels. The consultants believed a program could be developed that would achieve these ends and that would operate within the identified constraints, although the final product was not going to meet all the needs that Thompson had identified.

DESCRIBE OUTPUTS

- Identify output type.
- Identify output rate.

The system to be created will have to output certain products in order for its receiving systems to have the necessary inputs that will lead to goal attainment.

Example: Adams felt that the proposed program could meet the two stated goals by outputting the following:

Output No. 1: A weekly posting (in graphic form) of the absenteeism and tardiness rates of sales and marketing personnel, along with the average of the rest of the company for that same week; in addition, it would be necessary to output the message that dropping below the company average was desirable.

Output No. 2: Instruction and monitoring of management personnel so that they would verbally praise employees when Goal No. 2 was approached.

Output No. 3: Sales representatives who could set production objectives (sales representatives would call them "goals") and use graphic feedback to monitor progress toward goals

Output No. 4: Instruction and monitoring of managers so that they would verbally praise sales representatives for setting production objectives, maintaining feedback graphs, and improving their production.

Output No. 5: Individuals from the marketing department who had completed a stress assessment strategy and identified and practiced techniques that would reduce stress and its effects

Output No. 6: A monthly posting (in graphic form) of the level of stress-related health problems of the sales and marketing staffs, along with the average of the rest of the company for that same month

ANALYZE THE EXTERNAL NETWORK

- Identify second, third, and higher order receiving systems.
- Identify potential impact on receiving systems.
- Identify the intervening systems.
- Estimate the feasibility of achieving system goals, in light of external network information.

Before identifying the nature of the prospective system, it is necessary to make several external network considerations. The higher order receiving systems and intervening systems must be identified. This is shown in diagram form in Figure 9.2. If the impact on the system network will be too great or if intervening systems will prevent the attainment of goals, the feasibility of the prospective system must be questioned and a decision made as to whether or not to continue systems development.

Example: Adams and Thompson thought that the proposed outputs would not have significant impact on any systems beyond the first order receiving systems, which were the marketing and sales groups. Certain employee families (second order systems) might benefit from the reduction of stress on the employee, but this was not an issue with which the consultants needed to be concerned.

IDENTIFY ALTERNATIVE SYSTEMS AND/OR SUBSYSTEMS FOR PRODUCING SYSTEM OUTPUTS AND ACHIEVING GOALS

- Identify for each alternative system or subsystem,
  —the process necessary to produce outputs.

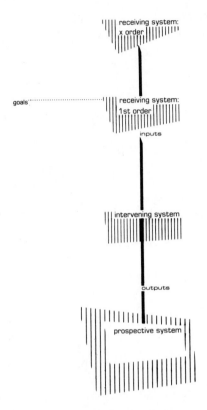

FIGURE 9.2   System design after completion of item
5 of the design outline.

—the components necessary for each process.
—the necessary subsystem configurations.
● Identify the constraints on the prospective system.
● Select the system(s) and/or subsystem(s) in which goal attainment is
maximized and constraints are minimized.

The outputs that the prospective system must produce can result
from a number of different subsystems. This step calls for the identification of those alternative means. In order to emphasize the breadth
of the possibilities here, it is suggested that even the creation of more
than one system be considered. Once the alternative system(s) or sub-
system(s) have been identified and developed, it is necessary to identify
the constraints that limit the feasibility of the various alternatives.
The system process selected may produce more outputs than just those
needed to achieve goals. If this is the case, one would need to consider the

impact of those additional outputs on each aspect of the system network. Figure 9.3 illustrates three alternative processes and impinging constraints.

Figure 9.4 shows that, in this particular example, a three-step process was selected for the system because it maximized the possibilities of attaining system goals, given the constraints. At this time, the details of the behavioral systems can be analyzed and described. Flowcharts at various levels of specificity are prepared, and once appropriate behaviors and decisions are identified, the discriminative and reinforcing stimuli as well as the contingencies can be stated.

Example: In the plan that Adams and Thompson developed, an assistant personnel supervisor was the major component (called the feedback

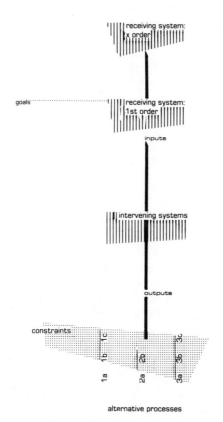

FIGURE 9.3   System design after partial completion of item 6 of the design outline.

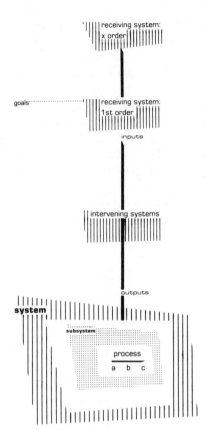

FIGURE 9.4   System design after completion of item
6 of the design outline.

program coordinator) in a two-step process that: (1) collected weekly data
from every department on the number of employees absent or tardy
during the previous five days and (2) prepared graphic feedback charts
that were prominently posted in the marketing department. The feedback
program coordinator also collected monthly medical data from the company physician and posted graphic feedback charts. Another assistant
from the personnel department (called the stress program director)
offered short programs to individuals so that they could learn to: (1) set
goals and utilize self-designed feedback graphs and (2) analyze types of
stress (physical, mental, emotional) along with stressors (those things
placing response demands upon the individual) and identify appropriate
stress reduction techniques (delegation, time management, recreation,
progressive relaxation, and so forth). The latter, short programs dealing

with stress management were structured to be a separate subsystem from the data collection and feedback subsystem. The role of the consultants was to prepare the necessary materials, train the people in the personnel department who would manage the two subsystems, and aid in the implementation and evaluation of the program. Before selecting this particular process for the system, Thompson and Adams considered the following alternative processes:

1. Establish a new Office of Environmental Management that would be abolished in 12 months. It would be staffed by a stress and behavior management specialist and an assistant. It would carry out the functions of the subsystems mentioned above, but in addition, it would gradually prepare specified managers to take over and continue the program beyond the 12-month life of the office.
2. Offer a series of in-service workshops (designed and planned by the consultants) in which the skills of feedback presentation and stress management would be developed in selected employees.
3. A combination of 1 and 2 above could be established so that currently employed managers could learn and implement feedback and reinforcement techniques, while stress management workshops would be conducted with the aid of experts in the field. The progress of the project could be monitored by the Office of Environmental Management.

The "low budget" and "low priority" constraints seemed to impact negatively on all three of the alternatives for achieving the specified goals. At this time Thompson and Adams began to recognize a philosophical constraint that they were imposing on the project, namely, that the program they developed should have some long-range effect rather than terminating once the consultants were no longer available. This meant that a certain amount of the budget would have to be allotted to follow-up visits by the consultants over a space of 24 to 30 months. The plan that was finally adopted appeared to be a reasonable compromise between desired outcomes and apparent constraints.

Instructional materials, step-by-step procedures, checklists, and sample graphics were prepared and compiled by Thompson and Adams. They also designed a schedule of involvement for the feedback program coordinator and the stress program director so that progressive approximations toward independent management of the program could be reinforced.

SPECIFY INPUTS TO THE PROPOSED SYSTEM

- Describe input type.
- Identify input rate.

- Identify input sources.
- Identify constraints on the proposed inputs.

The backward progression stops with the identification of inputs and input source(s). The purpose for identifying input constraints is to recognize possible influences from resource and administrative factors before they hinder planned inputs.

Example: The materials and directions initially provided by Adams and Thompson were critical inputs of the proposed subsystems (now called the Feedback Project and the Stress Management Program). In addition, it would be necessary for the absence, tardiness, and stress-related health problems data to be inputted on a regular schedule so that feedback graphs could be outputted. Managers, sales representatives, and marketing personnel would also have to come to the two programs on a regular basis in order for the goals to be met. An obvious constraint on this latter input arose from the fact that upper management wanted these to be voluntary programs without monetary incentives. A publicity campaign and release-time for participation were concessions that the consultants hoped would insure a steady flow of inputs.

DEVELOP PROCESS FEEDBACK MECHANISM(S)

- Identify feedback type(s) needed.
- Identify feedback sensor(s).
- Identify feedback interval(s).
- Describe the feedback procedure(s).
- Identify constraints on planned process feedback.

The system being planned will need process feedback mechanisms in order for the decider to monitor and control the process taking place within the system. A set of outputs that the system should produce and a process for producing them have already been selected. Now, the behavior manager must develop a means for helping the decider know if the intended processes are actually occurring when and where they should. The pertinent questions to consider are:

- What information should management receive in order to evaluate whether or not the intended process is taking place?
- How will the information be secured?
- How can the necessary information be secured most easily and economically?
- How often should feedback be available to management in order to control processes?

- What are the steps in the procedure of getting the information fed back from sensor to decider?
- What are the critical levels or types of information that call for action from the decider?
- What are the possible resource and administrative constraints that may influence the planned process feedback mechanism?
- What revisions should be made on the planned feedback mechanism, in light of the constraints?

Example: The feedback program coordinator and the stress program director would manage the various processes within the separate subsystems and, therefore, should receive feedback about how and at what rate processes were being completed. Very detailed checklists had been developed by the consultants to guide individuals through each subsystem. Individuals could enter checks on these lists as they moved through the various subsystems, and the coordinator or director could use these as feedback. By having participants enter the data and time when a part of the process was finished, it would be easy to determine how rapidly and in what order the parts of each process were being completed. Both consultants agreed that the "absence," "tardiness," and "health data" collection and posting systems needed no process feedback. Neither consultant could identify a constraint that would prevent them from proceeding in this fashion.

DEVELOP OUPTUT FEEDBACK MECHANISMS

- Identify feedback type(s).
- Identify feedback sensor(s).
- Identify feedback interval(s).
- Identify desired performance level(s).
- Describe the feedback procedure(s).
- Identify constraints on planned output feedback.

Many of the questions asked previously to develop process feedback can be modified and also used effectively to develop output feedback. An important and distinguishing feature of output feedback is its negative nature (as was discussed in Chapter Six). In order for the decider to recognize that the system is (or is not) functioning as planned, there must be a desired output level for comparison with actual levels. Corrections can be made only if the decider knows how the system is currently functioning and how it should function. Obviously, earlier efforts at goal setting pay off now because all decisions about desired types and levels of output depend upon the goals to be achieved.

Example: You will recall that the planned outputs were:

Output No. 1: A weekly posting (in graphic form) of the absenteeism and tardiness rates of sales and marketing personnel, along with the average of the rest of the company for that same week; in addition, it would be necessary to output the message that dropping below the company average was desirable

Output No. 2: Instruction and monitoring of management personnel so that they would verbally praise employees when Goal No. 2 was approached

Output No. 3: Sales representatives who could set production objectives (sales representatives would call them "goals") and use graphic feedback to monitor progress toward goals

Output No. 4: Instruction and monitoring of managers so that they would verbally praise sales representatives for setting production objectives, maintaining feedback graphs, and improving their production

Output No. 5: Individuals from the marketing department who had completed a stress assessment strategy and identified and practiced techniques that would reduce stress and its effects

Output No. 6: A monthly posting (in graphic form) of the level of stress-related health problems of the sales and marketing staffs, along with the average of the rest of the company for that same month

Adams and Thompson suggested that no output feedback mechanisms were necessary for Output Nos. 1 and 6. By using behavioral rehearsal techniques, one could assess the ability of managers to use praise in a simulated situation, but beyond that, no evaluation would take place for Output Nos. 2 and 4 since the program would not have the resources nor the authority to monitor managers once the consultants had left the program. The behavioral objectives and performance measures associated with Output Nos. 3 and 5 would serve as the output feedback sensors that would given the supervisor an indication of the quality of the outputs being produced. Thompson and Adams were well aware that some of the performance measures that they had developed were not yet as valid as they would like them to be and that revisions would have to be made in the materials (especially in the case of the stress reduction techniques).

DEVELOP ENVIRONMENTAL
FEEDBACK MECHANISMS

- Identify feedback type(s).
- Identify feedback sensor(s).
- Identify feedback interval(s).
- Describe feedback procedure(s).
- Identify constraints on planned environmental feedback.

The function of environmental feedback is extremely important; it indicates whether or not goals have been met. There are a number of questions to consider during this phase of system planning:

- What information will the decider need in order to evaluate a shift in the receiving system from one state to another?
- What is the most efficient and least obtrusive means for gathering that information?
- What should be done to insure that the information is accurate and representative of the state variable identified in the system goals?
- At what intervals should information be fed back in order to maintain control over the system?
- What means will be used to get the feedback from the sensor to the decider?
- What criteria will the decider use to evaluate the progress of the system and whether or not changes should occur in system operation?
- What are the possible resource and administrative factors that would influence the operation of the proposed environmental feedback mechanism?
- If the proposed environmental feedback mechanism is revised to account for constraints identified above, what impact will those revisions have on the operation of the feedback mechanism and subsequently on the successful functioning of the system?

Figure 9.5 diagrammatically illustrates the entire system design, complete with input sources, inputs, process, outputs, intervening systems, receiving systems, process feedback, output feedback, and environmental feedback.

Example: You will recall that the goals of the program were:

Goal No. 1: Within 18 months of the initiation of a stress management program, the stress-related health problems of the sales and marketing staff would be no greater than the company average.

Goal No. 2: Within ten months of the initiation of a management

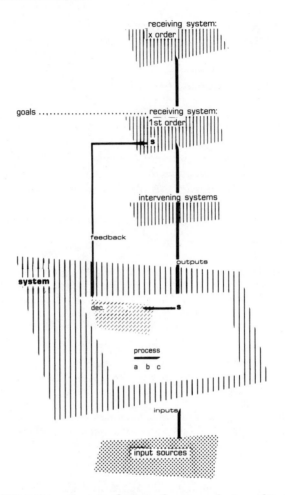

FIGURE 9.5   System design after completion of item
10 of the design outline.

program, absenteeism and tardiness of sales and marketing staff would decrease by 9 percent from baseline
figures (which would still exceed the company average).

Environmental feedback mechanisms for each of the two goals were
relatively easy for Adams and Thompson to develop. For Goal No. 1, the
necessary data for evaluation would already be collected and posted on a
monthly basis by the stress program director. That individual should be
able to recognize readily whether or not Goal No. 1 was being approached.
The same was true of the data needed for feedback regarding achieve-

ment of Goal No. 2. Weekly reports of absenteeism and tardiness were part of the process, and they could also be used for evaluation of the effect of the process and outputs. As an additional measure, the consultants recommended that both the feedback program coordinator and the stress program director receive the monthly productivity reports from the sales manager so that the programs' effects on current rates could be evaluated.

IDENTIFY POTENTIAL CONSTRAINTS ON THE ENTIRE SYSTEM

- Consider interactions or combinations of variables that may result in constraints.
- Consider system constraints that may arise from the system as a whole but not be indicated by any of its parts.

Finally, a last analysis of potential constraints upon the system is carried out before declaring the system design complete. The key concept associated with this final assessment of constraints is that "the whole is more than the sum of its parts." This is not to say that one would not have retained a wholistic view of the system throughout the planning and design procedure, but now that it is all together, a comprehensive overview should be attempted. By this time, the person designing the system should have a rather significant intellectual and emotional commitment to the plan that has evolved and, as a result, will have some difficulty identifying further constraints. Nevertheless, it is at this point that the true ecological makeup of the system is considered, and a last opportunity is available to plan for total system functioning.

Example: Both the feedback program coordinator and the stress program director were continuing to fulfill some regular duties in the personnel department. Thompson and Adams realized that the extent of those duties could severely limit the time available for this project. In addition, there was a well-disguised indication that many of the marketing and sales people believed that stress was an important part of their job, a crucial motivating factor as it were. This belief, coupled with the moderately low prestige of the personnel department within the plant, could prevent achievement of the goals. Things just might have stacked up against the program in a way that would have made failure inevitable. However, the company president was earnest in his support for the proposed program (even if he would not promote some internal changes that would have increased the probability of success), so the program was initiated as planned. With some careful nurturing and revisions to process, the goals were met, and the consultants were gratified to be offered the opportunity to extend the programs in the marketing department and to plan plant-wide system to achieve similar goals.

The entire system planning and design procedure is aimed at practical application, but the guidelines that follow should aid in avoiding some general pitfalls that can occur with the creation of a new system.

CHAPTER NINE: GUIDELINES FOR PRACTICAL APPLICATION

Guideline 9.1: If you are engaged by someone to design or plan a system, anticipate that the person or group for whom you are planning the system will either want a certain process to be carried out or will want a certain problem considered. Other things can stimulate system planning, but the "process or problem" focus is quite common.

—Expect some difficulty if a system is to be developed in order to carry out a particular process. More often than not, the individual or group favoring a particular process is assuming that a certain outcome will result from the process. It is unusual for anyone to be entirely unconcerned about outcomes. If you ferret out the desired outcome and perhaps suggest alternative processes for achieving those outcomes, you run the risk of irritating your client because that individual has told you what process is desired. On the other hand, if you simply set up a system that carries out the process, you may be faulted later because certain (implicit) outcomes did not occur. Remember: without desired outcomes, you cannot use feedback for evaluation and control.

—The situation in which you are called upon to plan and design a system because a problem exists is less troublesome than the "process focus" described above. The major difficulty to anticipate is that the client will already have some notions about what caused the problem and will expect you to pursue the "cause-effect" approach. You, of course, will move from a description of the problem to an analysis of desired outcomes. It may or may not be possible or useful to have some idea of the cause for the problem. Gentle guidance toward consideration of desired outcomes can be accomplished through well-phrased questions. Once you have a toehold on what outcomes your client desires, pursue them gently but firmly, returning to causes only when it may help you to achieve desired outcomes.

Guideline 9.2: Remember to stay flexible during the system planning and designing procedure. If you get locked into a particular process or structure, you may produce a system that is less effective (in relation to its goals) than it might have been. At some point, you will certainly have to settle on a particular design for the system, but until that point, give every new idea a chance to fit into the system.

TEN
ODDS AND ENDS

This final chapter will be devoted to a number of items that have been called "odds" and a few rather subjective observations that are the "ends." The odds are mostly explanations and examples of behavior management- and systems-related concepts and phenomena that enhance the use of the behavioral system framework but are not a part of the basic structure. Let us begin "odds" with a discussion of goals and subgoals.

ODDS

Goals, Multiple Goals, and Subgoals

The chapter on system goals could lead one to believe that a system has only one goal that it must rigidly and exclusively pursue. Of course, this is not the case. In many situations, long-range goals must be broken down into multiple short-range goals. This can involve a single sequence or a number of parallel goals that will eventually come together in the achievement of the final goal. An example of a single sequence of subgoals and a goal for a management consultant firm follows. The receiving system is Nova, Inc., a manufacturer that currently has a 90 percent turnover rate of its sales representatives every 5 years.

Goal: by December 31, 1985, Nova, Inc. will retain:

- 40 percent of the sales representatives that joined the firm in 1980.

- 55 percent of the sales representatives that joined the firm in 1981.
- 60 percent of the sales representatives that joined the firm in 1982 and 1983.
- 80 percent of the sales representatives that joined the firm in 1984.
- 95 percent of the sales representatives that joined the firm in the first 6 months of 1985.

Subgoals:

- By July 15, 1981, Nova, Inc. will have a fully operational selection system for sales representatives, based upon basic performance criteria.
- By June 1, 1982, Nova, Inc. will have a fully operational sales training program, based upon a behavioral and cognitive analysis and performance techniques.
- By December 15, 1983, Nova, Inc. will have a behaviorally based management program for sales representatives.

It should be obvious that even the subgoals have subgoals that involve, among other things, analyses, pilot studies, executive training, and establishment of performance files. However, the goals and subgoals presented are the primary benchmarks that will permit evaluation and control of the management consultant firm. The subgoals are considered to be sequential because each succeeding one is dependent upon some element or outcome of the preceding one. For instance, the selection system may result in the hiring of a small group of novice sales representatives who will not need training normally given to sales personnel. On the other hand, they may need training carried out in a certain way that usually is not part of traditional sales preparation. None of this inforation would be available until the selection system is operational; therefore, the development of the training program must come in sequence after the development of the selection program.

The subgoals would be regarded as parallel if all three programs— selection, training, and behavior management—could be developed concurrently and blended at some point for the achievement of the goal. Regardless of the task confronting the behavior management specialist, it is important to understand the specifics of subgoals and their relationships to each other.

The arrangement of goals and subgoals focusing on Nova, Inc. is such that conflicts are not likely to arise, but if multiple goals exist, the goals must be prioritized so that conflicts can be resolved easily. If the management consultant firm were to pursue the three subgoals and if each were to be achieved at the same time, multiple goals would exist and prioritizing would be a wise step.

Goals of Free Enterprise Systems

To the reader who is accustomed to looking at businesses in the United States, the concept of goals and especially the focus on receiving systems may appear to be a bit of a cockeyed notion. The purpose of a business is to make profits, and that has to take precedence over any concerns about the states of the receiving systems. Consequently, it would appear that the behavioral system framework is most appropriate for nonprofit and governmental organizations. Actually, the behavioral system framework can accommodate the free enterprise position very nicely and can prove quite valuable in its application.

The key to comprehending free enterprise businesses as open systems is to realize that all such operations have at least two goals. The first and most important goal focuses on the owner(s) or stockholders as a receiving system. The second goal is concerned with the clients or customers of the business.

By considering the owner or stockholders of a business to be a receiving system, it is possible to specify the desired level of income that the receiving system should have by an identified date. It may come in the form of a salary, bonus, or profit-sharing payment in the case of the owner(s) or in the form of dividends for stockholders. In order for the owner or stockholders to be in a certain financial state relative to the system specific monetary outputs will have to be produced by the system. Likewise, certain processes will have to be identified and carried out within the system.

Only the United States Treasury can produce money, so businesses must produce some other output that can be exchanged for money. Stated another way, the system needs to output money to one of its receiving systems (stockholders or owner), but restrictions necessitate that it input money rather than produce it. Thus, a producible output must flow to a second receiving system (customer or client) in exchange for money. If this description sounds a trifle contrived, consider the example of a goal focused upon the client receiving system that appeared in Chapter Six. It was stated as, "By October 15, 1982, Ski Enterprise will have and be knowledgeable about a complete environmental impact statement, which includes . . . (nine specific items to be assessed were listed.)"

Environmental Assessments, Inc. certainly was not planning to output an impact statement to Ski Enterprises for strictly altruistic purposes. The owner of Environmental Assessments, Inc. had another goal of having a net income of $38,000 from the corporation during that year. As is always the case with free enterprise, the latter goal of Environmental Assessments, Inc. depended upon the attainment of the former goal, although the latter was probably the major goal of the company.

Setting profit-oriented goals that focus on owners and stockholders as receiving systems is an unusual practice, especially among smaller organizations. It generally remains implicit that there is no upper limit on the needs of stockholders and owners. In practice, however, the setting of such goals allows for much more definitive planning than otherwise and permits the two functions of goals, to facilitate evaluation and control, to operate for the system. The value of profit-oriented goals was made evident to the author while consulting with a seven-member firm, when it was discovered that the owner/manager was satisfied with just breaking even after overhead expenses. After much discussion, he admitted that being able to occupy his plush, paneled office, eat lunch at the club, and go trout fishing when he wished was all that he wanted as a result of owning the business. His wife's income from the sale of her artwork was more than sufficient to support the family. The establishment of a behavior management program based upon the assumption that indefinitely increasing profits were desirable may have result in serious system problems. As it was, the identification of the owner/manager's actual desired state of the system permitted the use of bonuses and profit-sharing plans in a behavior management program that greatly enhanced the operation of the firm. As peculiar as it may seem, there are many systems that appear to operate within the domain of free enterprise yet do not seek increased profits as a primary outcome. For those systems in which increased profit is a major goal, the behavior manager should know how much is expected within a given time period.

The Principle of First and Second Order Measures

In Chapter Four, we discussed the identification of first and second order receiving systems in the external network of a system. The concept of first and second order measures that we are about to discuss should not be confused with first and second order receiving systems. They are not even related concepts.

However, the notion of first and second order measures is related to the idea of free enterprise systems having multiple goals. Basically, the Principle of First and Second Order Measure is as follows:

Whenever a behavior management program is carried out in an organization, at least two evaluative measures should be taken: (1) the first order measure assesses the impact of the behavior change on the attainment of the goals or values of the organization, and (2) the second order measure assesses the level of the behavior being managed.

An assumption associated with this principle is that behavior management in organizations is not carried out for its own sake. If the firm has goals, as discussed above, behavior management programs should be part of the system process leading to the attainment of those goals. It is possible that an organization could be operating in the absence of goals, in which case the decider's values may dictate that behavior management programs are more important than anything else. In such a situation, first and second order measures are identical; hence, only one measure is needed.

The logic for suggesting two measures is obvious, even in the face of a value-directed organization. Suppose that a behavior management specialist was consulted to work with the manager of the marketing department who is allegedly an unpleasant, critical, sullen person. The marketing agents have complained loudly enough to stimulate some action. Rather than transfer or release the marketing manager, his supervisor has decided to attempt a behavioral change program. Behavioral measures such as the frequency of saying "good morning," "please," "thank you," and praising work well done are identified, and baseline levels are obtained. The question should now be asked, "Why change the marketing manager's behavior?" His supervisor might say, "Well, because the people who work for him complained." However, that answer describes a possible cause for the behavior management program, and our question was aimed at effect. Asked another way, our question is, "What are you trying to achieve by changing the marketing manager's behavior?" There are a number of outcomes that the supervisor might suggest at this point, all of which could be the basis for a first order measure: "The marketing department would have a reduced turnover if the manager were more pleasant," or "The productivity of the marketing agents would go up if the manager were more pleasant," or "The marketing agents would complain less if the manager were more pleasant," or "The marketing department would be a happier place to work if the manager were more pleasant."

The only response from the supervisor that would make only one measure necessary would be: "We're not trying to achieve anything by changing the marketing manager's behavior. We simply want the behavior changed."

If the company officials are truly convinced that reduced turnover, greater productivity, fewer complaints, happier employees, or some other outcome is *not* the reason for the behavior management program, the behavior manager can continue to record only one type of measure and during spare time, reflect on the peculiar nature of the operation.

Goals of the Decider or Management Subsystem

Gall (1975) wrote a rather humorous and simplistic book in which a profusion of system laws, axioms, and principles appeared. Following his example, we shall state and discuss a formulation to be known as the Management Limit Law:

The Decider is not The System.

Throughout this book, we have referred to a subsystem called the *decider*. The decider is the executive or management subsystem of the parent system. As such, the function of the decider often necessitates that it output contingencies, directives, and memos to a variety of system components. It also often speaks for the system and, as a result, can be mistaken for being the system. A case of mistaken identity may not be a problem of any consequence unless the goals of the decider as a system itself (and as a subsystem of *The System*) are confused with the goals of *The System*. The problem, then, is rather straightforward; since the decider outputs to parts of its parent system or suprasystem, its goals can and should focus on the system of which it is a part. Explained another way, the system of which the decider is a part is also the receiving system of the decider subsystem.

If one mistakes the goals of the decider for the goals of the system, it will appear as if the goals of the system are focused on the system itself rather than on the receiving system. The confusion and attempts at revision that may result could eliminate functional goals and render the behavioral system framework unworkable at best. An example should clarify the issue. The management development center of a large computer company was drafting goals for the upcoming year.. The two following goals were suggested (among others):

1. The Central Atlantic, Southwest, and Ohio Valley management districts will have the rotating assignment scheduling procedure operating by October 1, 1977.
2. The management development center will have developed, evaluated, and have operational a two-day workshop on the rotating assignment scheduling procedure by January 1, 1977.

The first goal for the management development center, as a system, is appropriate. It focuses on three management districts as receiving systems. It is specific, manifest, and includes a time dimension. The second goal is not an appropriate goal for the management development center. It is an appropriate goal for the decider or manager(s) of the management development center system. As such, it is a vital, necessary goal and needs no revision. Visualize the management development center as currently being in State 1; no two-day workshop on rotating assignments is available. In order to meet the first goal, it must have such a workshop (State 2). The decider (management) of the management development center is responsible for outputting the proper directives to move the center from

State 1 to State 2. Therefore, the second goal stated was a management (decider) goal, not a system goal unless management is the system, which it is not.

Anytime that you encounter a goal that seems to focus on the system itself but that also appears to be a necessary outcome in order to meet some other acceptable goal, suspect that decider goals are being mistaken for system goals. Assign the goal in question to the decider or management function, and see if the fit is better than it was before.

ENDS

Colloquially, "ends," as in "odds and ends," probably refers to the last pieces from a bolt of cloth that are usually too good to throw away but not large enough to use profitably. The two items that follow have similar characteristics to bolt ends of cloth. For the purpose of this book, they should not be any larger, yet because behavioral management specialists will encounter them and perhaps effect some change, they are included as final observations about systems and human behavior.

A Process-Prone Society

There appears to be a tendency in the United States for people to immediately think of processes when problems arise. This predisposition to consider means before ends is part of a syndrome that could be called *process-proneness*. In addition to emphasis on means, this condition is also often characterized by a commitment or strong belief in the value of a certain methodology, regardless of accumulated supportive evidence or the lack of it. Hence, it seems that many of the systems that operate in our society do so on the basis of instrumental values or a preference for certain means rather than ends.

This situation would not be a problem if all processes had been evaluated and identified as clearly being most effective in achieving one or another end. Such evaluation and identification is impossible because of the infinite varying conditions that exist each time a problem appears. Each problem that we encounter will require a certain end state in order to be resolved, certain outputs will be necessary in order to achieve that end state, and certain processes will be necessary in order to output the required products, or so it would seem.

However, there are many examples of situations in which this logic does not prevail. Consider, for instance, the emphasis in education on methodology and the lack of interest in outcomes. Anyone who spends much time in a teacher's lunchroom or lounge within a school will hear extensive descriptions of new excercises, games, films, problems, and other techniques yet also hear very little discussion of the outcomes these means are meant to achieve. If outcome evaluation were prevalent, we could assume that the goals and objectives were well known but implicit. The lack of specific objectives and outcome evaluation in education, however, leads one to suspect that process is all-important while outcome is ignored. Education is not alone in this practice.

- Consider the Attica prison riot in New York in 1971. One of the conditions requested by inmates was that guards be given sensitivity training. To what end? What outcomes did the prisoners expect as a result of this process?
- Consider your local physician. The ends that you and the physician wish to achieve are usually implicit but reasonably well understood—the secession of pain or discomfort, the removal of an unsightly condition, or the assurance that no problems exist. Yet do you find that the two primary intervention processes, drugs and surgery, are always prescribed? With the rise of behavioral medicine, dietary counseling, and community preventive medicine programs, pharmacological and surgical intervention are not the only processes from which to select treatment procedures.
- Consider your local city government officials. Are they still discussing improved roads as the only process important to solving transportation problems? Have they identified transportation goals?
- Consider again our nation's prisons, where officials are complaining of the restrictions placed upon process while inmates are attempting to gain more freedom within the process. All the while, no one is entirely certain what the goals of our prisons are or what they should output to attain those goals.
- Consider socialized medicine. When such a system is described, do you hear information about the specific state of the receiving system (the population of the United States) vis-à-vis health or medical care? It is much more likely that you hear debates about how hospitals will be managed or how doctors will be paid or, in effect, how the process of the system will be carried out.

The list can go on to include most of our social, economic, govern-mental, and educational institutions. Business and industry are not im-mune to the practice of process-proneness, nor are churches or families. The effort needed to arrive at desired ends, identify necessary outputs, and evaluate alternative processes often seems too high a price to pay for the creation of a logically consistent system with the potential for self-correction. Yet recognition of the waste of economic, natural, and human resources resulting from process-proneness may provide the impetus for reassessment of the price of a systems approach.

A Note on Government Systems

During the past few years there has certainly not been any lack of criticism of government spending, regulation, and bureaucratic growth. The number of systems designed and/or funded by government in the

United States during the decade of the 1970s has probably been greater than in any similar period in the history of humanity. These systems have been accused of imposing an added burden on taxpayers, restricting the legitimate activity of business and industry, providing havens for the mediocre and incompetent, and deceiving the people for whom they were planned.

Have these government systems achieved their goals? Unfortunately, most of the government-created systems do not have goals, as we have defined them. In a very few cases, government programs have statements that purport to be goals but that, in fact, are vague descriptions of processes to be carried out. A smaller number have similar statements describing outputs to be produced. Almost none have specific statements focused on receiving systems. Thus, in most cases, they are goalless systems in which there is no evaluation in relation to receiving systems and no control other than that dictated by the instrumental values prevailing within the system. Is it any wonder, then, that government programs seem to have the sole purpose of perpetuating themselves?

Self-perpetuation, however, may not be the greatest danger that these systems represent for the people of the United States. There is a subtle deception being practiced that, in the long term, may seriously reduce whatever cohesion may exist among subgroups within our society. The deception may not spring from intentional dishonesty. It may even come about as the result of honest, well-meaning efforts being combined with an ignorance of the interactions occurring within social systems.

Nonetheless, the deception occurs, and it lies in the fact that receiving systems believe they are being aided by government-funded systems that merely carry out preferred processes. The mere allocation of funds and creation of systems that carry out certain processes are no guarantee of changes for the receiving system. To be deceived in this manner is to accept the premise that money and action, not outcomes, are sufficient to solve problems. Without prediction or knowledge of outcomes, government-supported systems can do as they wish and claim whatever seems most advantageous. Without goals that focus on receiving systems, there can be no evaluation or correction relative to desired ends.

Honest prediction and control over effects can come about through goal setting that focuses on the receiving system and requires specificity, but goal setting procedures of that nature would necessitate a needs assessment involving the people and systems affected. Compromises would be necessary when conflicts in values arose. The prospect of the majority disapproving of but paying for programs for the minorities might have to be accepted. Take, for instance, federal programs for minorities. What we have seen is the creation of systems that focus on processes in which black and Hispanic children practice behaving like white middle-class children. What do these systems output, and to which receiving systems? What is the desired state of the receiving system once this black child with the white behavior enters it? If we are talking about black families as receiving systems, what can we honestly predict about how this system will be different once it inputs a son or daughter so trained? Will the receiving system (family) want to achieve this new state? Whether we are talking about equal opportunities of minorities, support for small businesses, grants for cancer research, or endowments for the humanities, questions about proposed outputs, receiving systems, and outcomes are paramount to the honest, open design and to the operation of a truly effective system.

APPENDIX A
AN OUTLINE FOR ANALYZING
A BEHAVIORAL SYSTEM

1. Preliminary description of the system
   1.1 General boundary description
   1.2 General process description
   1.3 General function description
2. Goal analysis
   2.1 Identification of design goals
   2.2 Identification of currently operative goals
3. Scope of the system
   3.1 Input and output boundary structure and location description
   3.2 Input and output boundary conditions description
   3.3 Identification of receiving systems
4. Output ensemble specification
   4.1 Output type description
   4.2 Output rate (quantity/time) data
   4.3 Identification of nonselected outputs
5. Target Identification
   5.1 Identification of inferred receiving systems
       5.1.1 When goals exist
       5.1.2 In the absence of goals
   5.2 Inferred target specification
       5.2.1 Identification of state variables
       5.2.2 Identification of values of state variables
6. Input ensemble specifications
   6.1 Input type description
   6.2 Input rate (quantity/time) data
   6.3 Identification of input sources
7. System external network description

7.1 Arrangement of input source systems
7.2 Arrangement of receiving systems—first order
    7.2.1 Goal-related
    7.2.2 Target-related
7.3 Identification of second, third, and higher order receiving systems
7.4 Identification of critical intervening systems
    7.4.1 Process description
    7.4.2 Function description
    7.4.3 Identification of intersystem contingencies
7.5 Description of suprasystems
8. Process description
  8.1 Identification of components
  8.2 Identification and description of subsystems
    8.2.1 Identification of subsystem inputs and outputs
    8.2.2 Identification of subsystem networks
  8.3 Process time data
  8.4 Behavioral subsystem description
    8.4.1 Flowchart description
      8.4.1.1 Identification of mission phases, operational functions, and unit operations*
    8.4.2 Behavioral description
      8.4.2.1 Identification of reinforcers
      8.4.2.2 Identification of discriminative stimuli
      8.4.2.3 Identification of contingencies
9. Analysis of process feedback mechanisms
  9.1 Description of sensor
  9.2 Description of feedback type
  9.3 Identification of feedback interval (frequency)
10. Analysis of output feedback mechanisms
  10.1 Description of sensor
  10.2 Description of feedback type
  10.3 Identification of feedback interval (frequency)
  10.4 Identification of desired performance level
11. Analysis of environmental feedback mechanisms
  11.1 Goal-related receiving system feedback
    11.1.1 Description of sensor
    11.1.2 Description of feedback type
    11.1.3 Identification of feedback interval (frequency)
  11.2 Target-related receiving system feedback

---

*Mission phases, operational functions, and unit operations are parts of a three-level analysis technique in which unit operations correspond to the flowcharting described in Chapter Five. The reader should consult R. E. Corrigan & R. A. Kaufman, *Why System Engineering*, Belmont, Calif.: Fearon, 1966, for further details.

       11.2.1 Description of feedback type

       11.2.2 Identification of feedback interval (frequency)

       11.2.3 Description of feedback channel(s)

       11.2.4 Identification of relationship of feedback to system values

12. Identification of constraints on system

    12.1 Identification of resource constraints: economic, manpower, technological

    12.2 Identification of administrative constraints: philosophical, political, policy, procedural

APPENDIX B
AN OUTLINE FOR PLANNING AND DESIGNING A BEHAVIORAL SYSTEM

1. Needs Assessment
    1.1 Identification of receiving systems and social sets
    1.2 Identification of receiving system state variables to be changed or maintained
    1.3 Identification of current and desired values of state variables
    1.4 Identification of inputs necessary to achieve desired values of state variables
2. Identification of constraints
    2.1 Resource and administrative constraints that influence achievement of desired values of state variables
    2.2 Resource and administrative constraints that influence necessary inputs
3. Development of goals
    3.1 Estimation of time required to achieve each of the desired values of the receiving system state variables
    3.2 Compilation of desired values of receiving system state variables (Item 1.3) with estimation of required time to achieve the desired values (3.1)
    3.3 Comparison of goals in 3.2 with constraints identified in 2
4. Description of output ensemble
    4.1 Identification of output type (from Item 1.4)
    4.2 Identification of output rate
5. External network analysis
    5.1 Identification of second, third, and higher order systems
    5.2 Identification of potential impact on higher order systems
    5.3 Identification of intervening systems
    5.4 Estimation of the feasibility of achieving goals in 3, given 5.2 and 5.3

6. Identification of alternative systems and/or subsystems for producing the outputs in Item 4 and achieving the goals in Item 3
   6.1 For each alternative system or subsystem, identify:
      6.1.1 The process(es) necessary to produce the outputs
      6.1.2 The components necessary for each process in 6.1.1
      6.1.3 The necessary subsystem configurations
   6.2 Identification of the resource and administrative constraints on the prospective system
   6.3 Selection of the system(s) and/or subsystem(s) from 6 in which goal attainment is maximized and constraints are minimized
   6.4 Description of behavioral subsystem processes
      6.4.1 Flowchart description
      6.4.2 Behavioral description
7. Input ensemble specifications
   7.1 Description of necessary input type
   7.2 Identification of input rate
   7.3 Identification of input sources
   7.4 Identification of constraints on proposed inputs
8. Development of process feedback mechanism(s)
   8.1 Identification of feedback type(s) needed
   8.2 Identification of feedback sensor(s)
   8.3 Identification of feedback interval(s)
   8.4 Description of feedback procedure
   8.5 Identification of constraints on planned process feedback
9. Development of output feedback mechanism(s)
   9.1 Identification of feedback type(s) needed
   9.2 Identification of feedback sensor(s)
   9.3 Identification of feedback interval(s)
   9.4 Identification of desired performance level(s)
   9.5 Description of feedback procedure(s)
   9.6 Identification of constraints on planned output feedback
10. Development of environmental feedback mechanism(s)
   10.1 Identification of feedback type(s) needed
   10.2 Identification of feedback sensor(s)
   10.3 Identification of feedback interval(s)
   10.4 Description of feedback procedure(s)
   10.5 Identification of constraints on planned environmental feedback
11. Identification of constraints on the entire system
   11.1 Consideration of interactions and combinations that may result in constraints
   11.2 Consideration of whole/part aspects that may result in constraints

BIBLIOGRAPHY

Angyal, A. *Foundations for a science of personality*. Cambridge: Harvard University Press, 1941.

Ashby, W. R. General systems theory as a new discipline. *General Systems Yearbook*, 1958, *3*, 1–6.

Bacon-Pure, A., Blount, R., Pickering D., & Drabman, R. An evaluation of three litter control procedures: Trash receptacles, paid workers, and the marked item techniques. *Journal of Applied Behavior Analysis*, 1980, *13*, 165–170.

Baer, D. M., Wolf, M. M., & Risley, T. R. Some current dimensions of applied behavior analysis. *Journal of Applied Behavior Analysis*, 1968, *1*, 91–97.

Beckett, J. A. *Management Dynamics*, New York: McGraw-Hill, 1971.

Beishon, J. *Systems*. Buckinghamshire: The Open University Press, 1972.

Berelson, B., & Steiner, G. A. *Human Behavior*. New York: Harcourt, Brace & World, 1964.

Berrien, F. K. *General and social systems*. New Brunswick: Rutgers University Press, 1968.

Bertalanffy, L. V. *General system theory*. New York: George Braziller, 1968.

Brethower, D. M. *Behavioral analysis in business and industry: A total performance system*. Kalamazoo, Mich.: Behaviordelia, 1972.

Churchman, C. W. *The systems approach*. New York: Dell Publishing, 1968.

Cone, J. D., & Hayes, S. C. *Environmental problems/behavioral solutions*. Monterey, Calif.: Brooks/Cole, 1980.

Corrigan, R. E., & Kaufman, R. A. *Why systems engineering*. Belmont, Calif.: Fearon, 1966.

Crowder, D. M., Bennett, A. C. Total commitment to goals is secret of hospital's success. *Hospitals*, *50*, 104–109, 1976.

Cyert, R. M., & March, J. G. *A behavioral theory of the firm*. Englewood Cliffs, N.J.: Prentice-Hall, 1963.

DeGreene, K. *Systems psychology*. New York: McGraw-Hill, 1970.

Doleys, D. M., Stacy, D., & Knowles, S. Modification of grooming behavior in adult retarded: Token reinforcement in a community-based program. *Behavior Modification*, 1981, 5, 119–128.

Easton, D. *A systems analysis of political life*. New York: John Wiley & Sons, 1961.

Emery, F. E., & Trist, E. L. Socio-technical systems. In C. W. Churchman & M. Yerhulst (Eds.), *Management science, models and techniques* (Vol. 2). Elmsford, N. Y.: Pergamon, 1960.

Ferster, C. B., Culbertson, S., & Boran, Mary P. *Behavior principles*. Englewood Cliffs, N.J.: Prentice-Hall, 1975.

Fischer, J., & Gochros, H. L. *Planned behavior change*. New York: MacMillan, 1975.

Forrester, J. W. *Principles of systems*. Cambridge, Mass.: Wright-Allen Press, 1968.

Frisch, K. B. Decoding the language of the bee. *Science*, 1974, *23*, 663–668.

Gall, J. *Systemantics*. New York: Pocket Books, 1975.

Haberstroh, C. Control as an organizational process. *Management Science*, 1965, *6*, 165–171.

Hall, A. D., & Fagan, R. E. Definition of system. In W. Buckley (Ed.), *Modern systems research for the behavioral scientist*. Chicago: Aldine, 1968.

Hayes, S. C., & Cone, J. D. Reduction of residential electricity use: Information, payments, and feedback. *Journal of Applied Behavior Analysis*, 1977, *10*, 425–435.

Hayes, S. C., & Cone, J. D. Reduction of residential consumption of electricity through simple monthly feedback. *Journal of Applied Behavior Analysis*, 1981, *14*, 81–88.

Hilgard, E. L. R. *Theories of learning*. New York: Appleton-Century-Crofts, 1956.

Hodge, P. The application of general systems theory to secondary education. In A. J. Romisyowski, *The systems approach to education and training*. London: Kogan Page, 1970. (Taken from J. Beishon, *Systems*. Buckinghamshire: The Open University Press, 1971.)

Holder, H. O., & Stratas, N. E. A systems approach to alcoholism programming. *American Journal of Psychiatry*, 1972, *129*, 32–37.

Hughes, G. D., Rao, V. R., & Aiker, H. A. The influence of values, information, and decision orders on a public policy decision. *Journal of Applied Social Psychology*, 1976, *6*, 145–158.

Jones, J. C. The designing of man-machine systems. In W. T. Singleton et al. (Eds.), *The human operator in complex systems*. London: Taylor and Francis, 1967.

Kazdin, A. E. Recent advances in token economy research. In M. Hersen, R. Eisler, and P. M. Miller (Eds.), *Progress in behavior modification*. New York: Academic Press, 1975.

Kazdin, A. E. *Behavior modification in applied settings*. Homewood, Ill.: Dorsey, 1980.

Kazdin, A. E., & Geesey, S. Enhancing classroom attentiveness by preselection of back-up reinforcers in a token economy. *Behavior Modification*, 1980, *4*, 98–114.

Klir, G. J. (Ed.). *Trends in general systems theory*. New York: John Wiley & Sons, 1972.

Kohlenberg, R., & Phillips, T. Reinforcement and rate of litter depositing. *Journal of Applied Behavior Analysis*, 1973, *6*, 391–396.

Kohlenberg, R., Phillips, T., & Proctor, W. A behavioral analysis of peaking in residential electrical-energy consumer. *Journal of Applied Behavior Analysis*, 1976, *9*, 13–19.

Laszlo, C. A., Levine, M. D., & Milsum, J. H. A general systems framework for social systems. *Behavioral Science*, 1974, *19*, 79–91.

Laszlo, E. *The systems view of the world*. New York: George Braziller, 1972.

Leitenberg, H., Agras, W. S., Thompson, L. E., & Wright, D. E. Feedback in behavior modification: An experimental analysis in two phobic cases. *Journal of Applied Behavior Analysis*, 1968, *1*, 131–138.

Mager, R. F. *Preparing instructional objectives*. Belmont, Calif.: Fearon, 1965.

Mager, R. F. *Goal analysis*. Belmont, Calif.: Fearon, 1972.

Martin, G., & Pear, J. *Behavior modification: What it is and how to do it*. Englewood Cliffs, N.J.: Prentice-Hall, 1978.

Mayr, O. The origins of feedback control. *Scientific American*, 1970, *223*, 4, 110–118.

McConnell, J. V. Psycho-technology and personal change. In M. Seigal & H. Ziegler (Eds.), *Psychological research: The inside story*. New York: Harper & Row, 1976.

McInnis, R., & Kitson, L. Process and outcome evaluation in mental health systems. *International Journal of Mental Health*, 1977, *5*, 58–72.

Millenson, J. R. *Principles of behavioral analysis*. New York: MacMillan, 1967.

Miller, J. G. Living systems: Basic concepts. *Behavioral Science*, 1965a, *10*, 193–237.

Miller, J. G. Living systems: Structure and process. *Behavioral Science*, 1965b, *10*, 337–379.

Miller, J. G. Living systems: Cross-level hypotheses. *Behavioral Science*, 1965c, *10*, 380–411.

Miller, J. G. *Living systems*. New York: McGraw-Hill, 1977.

Morasky, R. L. Defining goals: A systems approach. *Long Range Planning*, 1977, *10*, 85–89.

Morasky, R. L. *Learning disabilities*. Boston: Allyn & Bacon, 1980.

Morasky, R. L., & Amick, D. Social systems needs assessment. *Long Range Planning*, 1978, *11*, 47–54.

O'Neill, G. W., Blanck, L. S., & Johner, M. A. The use of stimulus control over littering in a natural setting. *Journal of Applied Behavior Analysis*, 1980, *13*, 379–381.

Page, T. J., Iwata, B. A., & Neef, N. A. Teaching pedestrian skills to retarded persons: Generalization from the classroom to the natural environment. *Journal of Applied Behavior Analysis*, 1976, *9*, 433–444.

Parsegian, V. I. *This cybernetic world of men, machines and earth systems*. Garden City, N.Y.: Doubleday, 1972.

Parsons, T. Suggestions for the sociological approach to a theory of organizations—I. *Administrative Science Quarterly*, 1956, *1*, 63–85.

Quilitch, H. R. A comparison of three staff-management procedures. *Journal of Applied Behavior Analysis*, 1975, *8*, 59–67.

Reese, E. P., Howard, J., & Reese, T. W. *Human behavior: Analysis and application*. Dubuque, Iowa: W. C. Brown, 1978.

Reynolds, G. S. *A primer of operant conditioning*. Glenview, Ill.: Scott, Foresman, 1968.

Robinson, P. W., Newby, T. J., & Ganzell, S. L. A token system for a class of under-achieving hyperactive children. *Journal of Applied Behavior Analysis*, 1981, *14*, 307–316.

Rogers, C. R., & Skinner, B. F. Some issues concerning the control of human behavior: A symposium. *Science*, 1956, *124*, 1057–1066.

Rokeach, M. *The nature of human values*. New York: The Free Press, 1973.

Rosenbleuth, A., Weiner, N., & Bigelow, J. Behavior, purpose and teleology. *Philosophy of Science*, 1943, *10*, 18–24.

Ross, R. R., & Price, M. J. Behavior modification in corrections: Autopsy before mortification. *International Journal of Criminology and Penology*, 1976, *4*, 305–315.

Seaver, W., & Vernon, J. Decreasing fuel-oil consumption through feedback and social commendations. *Journal of Applied Behavior Analysis*, 1976, *9*, 147–153.

Simon, H. A. *The sciences of the artificial*. Cambridge: MIT Press, 1969.

Skinner, B. F. *Science and human behavior*. New York: MacMillan, 1953.

Slavin, R. E., Wodarski, J. S., & Blackburn, B. L. A group contingency for electricity conservation in master-metered apartments. *Journal of Applied Behavior Analysis*, 1981, *14*, 357–363.

Sommerhoff, G. The abstract characteristics of living systems. In F. E. Emergy (Ed.), *Systems thinking*. Baltimore: Penguin, 1969.

Thomas, E. J. (Ed.) *Behavior modification procedure: A sourcebook*. Chicago: Aldine, 1974.

Thompson, J. D. *Organizations in action*. New York: McGraw-Hill, 1967.

Thompson, M. A. A systems approach to environmental engineering. *Behavioral Science*, 1975, *20*, 306–326.

Weinberg, G. M. *An introduction to general systems thinking*. New York: John Wiley & Sons, 1975.

Weiner, N. *Cybernetics: Or control and communication in the animal and the machine*. Cambridge: MIT Press, 1961.

Winett, R. A., Kaiser, S., & Haberkorn, G. The effects of monetary rebates and feedback on electricity conservation. *Journal of Environmental Systems*, 1977, *6*, 329–241.

Winett, R. A., & Neale, M. S. Flexible work schedules and family time allocation: Assessment of a system change on individual behavior using self-report logs. *Journal of Applied Behavior Analysis*, 1981, *14*, 39–46.

Winett, R. A., Neale, M. S., & Grier, H. C. Effects of self-monitoring and feedback on residential energy consumption. *Journal of Applied Behavior Analysis*, 1979, *12*, 173–184.

Winkler, R. C. Reinforcement schedules for individual patients in a token economy. *Behavior Therapy*, 1971, *2*, 534–537.

Witmer, J. F., & Geller, E. S. Facilitating paper recycling: Effects of prompts, raffles, and contests. *Journal of Applied Behavior Analysis*, 1976, *9*, 315–322.

Young, R. C. Goals and goal setting. *Journal of American Institute of Planners*, 1966, *32*, 78–86.

Yuchtman, E., & Seashore, S. E. A system resource approach to organizational effectiveness. *American Sociological Review*, 1967, *32*, 891–903.

GLOSSARY

Channel: a discrete path through a system or portion of a system, limited by its capacity to process signals. Examples: the official entrances into a national park are channels for inputs and outputs and roads are channels for moving people through the park; the channels for inputs to an executive may be the telephone, mail, and personal contacts; if a regulatory agency systematically deals with all requests in one of four different ways, each of the four is a channel.

Components: a general term referring to the parts of a system. Examples: the traffic and criminal bureaus could be components of a police department; parents are one component of a family—the mother and father are components of the component, parents, of the system, family (see Guideline 2.3).

Contingencies: if/then relationships existing between behaviors and consequences. Examples: if the administrative assitant always has memos on the administrator's desk on time, then that person will not be criticized for late work; this is a contingency that could exist in an office. A contingency for a small business development program might be: if the proposal outline is completed accurately, then program officials will help the client locate financial support.

Decider: the part of every system that performs the management or executive function, such as determining input/output boundary conditions, process, feedback mechanisms, and component selection. (Keep in mind that the decider is an activity or a function, not a person.) The decider function can be (and often is) performed or shared by more than one individual. Examples: the decider function of a prison determines the type and number of inmates entering the prison, the treatment received by inmates in the prison, the type and number of parolees released from the prison, and the number and type of staff employed within the prison. Note that some of the decisions in the prison example would be made by the warden, some by the parole board, some by judges passing sentences, and some by government officials such as the governor.

Discriminative Stimuli: things in the environment that you have learned to recognize as signals for certain consequences. Examples: rising (feeding) trout are a signal (discriminative stimulus) that a hooked fish should occur (pleasant consequence) if an artificial fly is laid appropriately upon the water; a client's nod of agreement is a signal that, if offered the contract now, he will sign and accept the proposed terms; a malfunctioning gauge is a signal that the operation should be stopped before loss of coolant occurs.

Environmental Feedback: information to system managers about the effects of system outputs on receiving systems. If goals exist, this information will relate to the specific conditions expressed in the goals. Examples: the dean of a business school will receive information from companies about how well graduates of the school are performing specific tasks in the companies; the fire chief will receiving information from a house-to-house survey, indicating the impact that a radio and newspaper campaign has had on home fire safety measures; a garbage collection company will get feedback from customers about the neatness and promptness of pickup.

Feedback: information coming to a system about various state variables within the system and within the receiving systems. Examples: officials of a prison (system) may get information (feedback) about the number of parolees (outputs) gainfully employed (state variable) in a particular community (receiving system); a manager (subsystem) of a department store (system) may get information (feedback) about the number of salesclerks (state variable) and special sales (state variable) during rush hour.

Feedback Sensor: the device used to secure and feed information back to system management. Examples: an electronic counter senses the number of cars leaving a national park (output) and feeds the information to a computer that permits a set of number of entrance passes to be sold; a counselor (sensor) visits the job sites (receiving system) of adult retardates from a "community living program" and gathers performance data, which the program director uses to guide further training; a color-coded case progress board (sensor) is updated at 12:00 and 5:00 P.M. by employees working on various apsects of contracts in a tax consultant firm.

First Order Receiving System: the receiving system that inputs directly from the system in question.

Inputs: the things that enter a system. Examples: students are inputs to the system called school; manuscripts are inputs to a printing company.

Input Source System: the source from which a system gets its inputs. Examples: a police department (system) gets requests for assistance (inputs) from the community (input source system); a land-use planning committee (system) gets petitions (inputs) from business (input source system); an electronic diagnosis training program within a company gets students from franchised agencies.

Mediated Feedback Loop: a process, output, or environmental feedback mechanism that has a human component for receiving the information and deciding the extent of the change (if any) in system process or output. In nonmediated loops the change occurs automatically. Examples: the director of a hospital laboratory got daily feedback on the rate at which reports left the lab; on one occasion he immediately changed a procedure when 18-hour delays occurred, yet on another occasion he waited 2 additional days to see if 12-hour delays would continue.

Needs Assessment: a method for determining what inputs should be available to a receiving system in order for it to achieve desired states. Examples: a needs assessment for a program for the handicapped would determine what the program should input in order to achieve desired ends among the handicapped people that it services; a needs assessment for poverty-level families would find out what states the families should be in and would identify the inputs necessary to achieve those states.

Outputs: the things that leave a system. Examples: traffic citations are outputs from a police department; books are outputs from a printing company.

Output Feedback: information flowing to system managers about the outputs leaving the system. Examples: the director of an employment training program will receive output feedback regarding how many students leave the program per week and what their specific skills are; the captain of a police department will receive weekly reports on how many citations were issued, how many arrests were made, and how many times assistance was given to citizens.

Process: the events that take place within the system to change inputs to outputs. Example: the medical treatment and care on a pediatrics ward between the time a child enters with an illness and leaves in good health is the process of that system.

Process Feedback: information flowing to system managers about the process being carried out within the system. Such information may include the rate at which certain tasks are done, how well they are done, the method used, and so forth. Examples: the director of a respiratory diseases treatment center will receive process feedback indicating how often inhalation therapy was given, by whom, and what the effects were; process feedback to the manager of a financial advisory group will include the stage or progress of each case, who is currently doing what on the case, what method is being used to calculate investment returns, and so forth.

Receiving System: the system to which outputs go. There may be several receiving systems for a given system. Some receiving systems may be labeled "intended receiving systems" to indicate that the intent of the system was that outputs would flow to a specific or "intended" receiving system. Examples: subscribers and readers are the receiving systems for the system, daily newspaper; community families are the receiving systems for fire safety instruction (output) from the system, fire department.

Reinforcing Stimuli: consequences that follow a behavior and increase or decrease the frequency of subsequent occurrences of that behavior. Pleasant consequences tend to increase the behavior that they follow while aversive consequences tend to decrease the behavior that they follow. The loss of an order was an aversive consequence (reinforcing stimulus) that decreased the salesman's behavior of using the client's nickname without invitation to do so; praise from a superior was a pleasant consequence that increased the behavior of proper tool use on the part of a road gang laborer.

Second Order Receiving System: the receiving system that receives inputs from the first order receiving system. A second order receiving system is once removed from *the system*. Examples: a jobs training program (the system) may output graduates with basic skills to a technical training center (first order receiving system), which in turn will output these same persons to a job setting (second order receiving system); a law firm (the system) may output tax law interpretations to a financial advisor (first order receiving system), who will in turn use the information to output financial plans for clients (second order receiving system).

Signal: a general label for the thing that is passing through a system. Examples: a patient in a medical clinic; an income tax report in an IRS office; a participant in a workshop; an inmate in a correctional center.

State Variable: a part of a system that can assume different values. Examples: state variables of a prison could be inmate population (350 minimum to 800 maximum), number of guards (105 minimum to 270 maximum), number of recreation minutes per week for inmates (0 minimum to 21 hours maximum).

Subsystem: that portion of a larger system that carries out a specific task or function. Examples: the traffic bureau is a subsystem of the system, police department; the "meal preparation operation" is a subsystem of the system, family.

Suprasystem: the next larger system in which a system is embedded or nested. Examples: if the surgery ward is the system being examined, city/county hospital is the suprasystem; if the sales management section is the system being examined, the marketing department is the suprasystem.

System: a structure of interacting animate and inanimate parts that receives inputs and produces outputs. Examples: police department, school, printing company, family, group home, pediatrics ward.

System Goal: a manifest statement that describes the specific state a receiving system should attain by a specified time. Goals facilitate evaluation and control of systems. Examples: for a fire department, within 12 months the community will have 40 percent fewer fires than the average for the past 5 years; for a jobs training program, within 12 months community businesses will employ 12 of the 15 adolescents currently being trained.

System Network: a string or sequence of systems connected by input/output flows. At the minimum, such sequences include *the system* under examination, the input source system, and the receiving system. There is no maximum number of systems that can be interconnected. Example: parts of a "beef production network" include the feeder lot as the system under examination, ranches as the input source systems, and meat packing houses or slaughterhouses as the receiving systems.

System State: A condition displayed by a system that is usually associated with one or more state variables. Examples: a real estate sales system could be in state A, wherein it has more than 100 residences for sale or in state B, wherein it has fewer than 100 residences for sale; a family could be in state A wherein arguments occur nightly, in state B wherein arguments occur weekly, or in state C wherein arguments occur on the average of once a month.

System Values: the hierarchy of preferred system and receiving system states. Such values reside with the decider function and may or may not coincide with goals. Examples: the three supervising nurses (decider function) of the geriatrics ward (system) often seem to prefer that the patients be lying down and nondisruptive during social hour (value) rather than ambulatory and engaged in discussion (goal); the social workers (decider) in an urban nutrition improvement program (system) without specific goals seem to prefer that the clients (receiving system) eat three times a day (value A) more than other outcomes, such as eating balanced meals (value B) or eating natural or unprocessed foods (value C).

Target: an outcome or state that a system is approaching that is not described in the system's goals. If the system has no goals, all outcomes that it approaches are targets. Examples: a system may be set up to increase citizen participation in land-use planning but actually outputs materials that bias citizens against mobile home subdivisions (target); a system may be designed to increase the number of small businesses owned by minority group individuals in a community (goal) but actually increases the size of existing medium-sized businesses owned by nonminority group individuals (target); a government agency without goals may be doing little more than increasing its budget, its staff, and its record file (targets).

INDEX

ABOUT THE AUTHOR

Robert L. Morasky is a Professor of Psychology at Montana State University. He received his doctorate in 1968 from the University of Michigan where he specialized in applied learning theory. His introduction to behavior management and general systems theory occurred while doing graduate studies and the years since have seen a gradual synthesis of the two areas into the behavioral systems conceptual framework. His extensive consultant work in the public and private sectors has provided the necessary practical experience to understand the problems and needs of management. "Early in my professional career I saw a need for a conceptual framework or some type of tool for placing behavior in the context of the system in which it occurred. Since behavior did not occur in isolation, it did not seem reasonable to attempt to manage it in isolation." Having published numerous books and articles in the areas of behavior management and systems, Professor Morasky is well qualified to present this informative and useful book for those who are responsible for managing, evaluating, analyzing, and planning programs involving human behavior. An avid skier and fly fisherman, his life in the Rocky Mountains is a pleasant compromise between his love for the outdoors and his strong interest in problem solving in organizations.

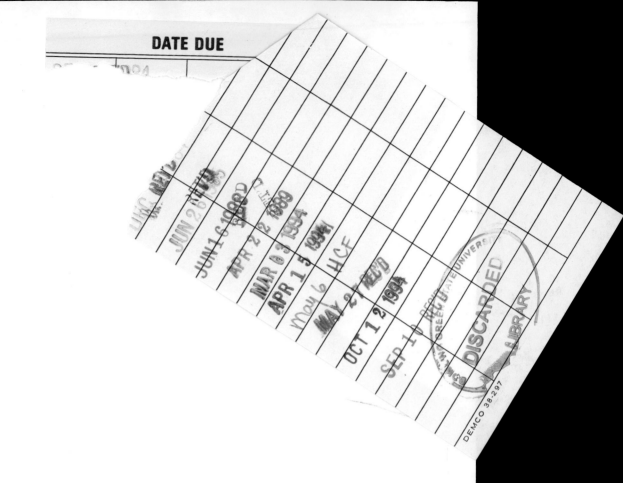